I0149546

i

forged by fire

PANDORA PRESS

Forged by Fire
Copyright © 2013 Pandora Press
ISBN: 0615764452

Pandora Press
15351 Hwy 5
Cabot, AR 72023

for the world,
in hopes it someday understands

Acknowledgements

There are so few ways to convey appropriate thanks when it comes to a project of this magnitude. It began in 2011 as a tiny seedling dream in the mind of one poet, who gathered many of us together, selecting varied wildflowers out of a tangled field. Those flowers spread roots, gathering yet more together, and this book blossomed as a unique, never before seen bouquet.

It may not seem like a much, a compilation of thirteen authors and poets and artists, but when you take into account thirteen different individuals from across the globe, a vast range of ages, experiences, and walks of life, not to mention thirteen different opinions…there were many who said it could not be done.

All functions in the creation of this book can be credited to the thirteen poets within it. Their contributions span not only the written word, but the cover art, editing process, and publication of this work. Without each one volunteering their time and talents, this could not have been accomplished. Blessings, thanks, and a roaring applause to all of you for your patience, your fortitude, and your beautiful ability to compromise.

A special thanks is due to Nancy Alcorn, who kept the fires burning when it seemed that the blaze of this project had guttered to embers. Thank you for your steadfast encouragement and consistent optimism and belief in this book.

Our especial gratitude to Elizabeth George, who was instrumental from the beginning; gathering together poetry, edits, answering a slew of questions, and keeping all apprised of the situation. Without her, this book could not have been made into a cohesive whole.

Yet another special thanks to Danté Camerlengo, whose beautiful poetry not only lies within these pages, but his artwork which graces the cover. Thank you for beautifying this book and making it a work of art in more ways than one.

Last but not least, a thanks to Evadne Anderson, who dedicated her time and resources to the publication of this book so that we can see it in print, and realize this long-awaited dream.

TABLE OF CONTENTS

Foreword
by Nancy Alcorn

It is again 3 am and that part of me which needs, must sleep, is inflicting itself upon my fertile imagination, as though a bull whip were being applied to my hide.

It is at this moment the number 13 dances into my peripheral vision and plagues my half-wakened state with witticisms and riveting clarity. Yet, when I attempt to pen it all, it dissipates as the fog when the sun breaks through its soggy depths and glows in such a gleeful manner.

Which brings me to this; if you were to connect the dots between the poets in this book what would it show you? Would it map out a new planetary lesion or look like a lopsided lollapalooza? Or would it just be a squiggly line with no real focus or direction? No matter what it would look like, the poets within this book bring to life their thoughts, ideas, dreams, and perhaps nightmares.

In my view it is a collection that may not be the crème de la crème of the poet's world or even the best of the best, or the worst of the worst; it is a sampling of my favorite unknowns who were especially chosen not only for diversity but also to show that we could work together towards a common dream and bring it to completion.

From each of us our thanks, for picking us up to read and share in our sorrows, our joys, and our love of the written word. Remember, poetry is not dead. It is a life force pulsating at our wrists and pulling on our minds; it is the drumbeat that drives our ambitions.

We give you Forged by Fire.

forged by fire

and death stood down

by dave magill

See Me

I will not be the one that wept
while watching the landscape burn
I will not tell you about how I have loved
and been returned
the favor.
I will not bore you with my feelings
I will only suggest a picture for you,
a flower with blue fire
threatening its petals
as all else
has abandoned it.
I will offer you the green grass
at dawn
and ask that you see it
clearly.

Chlorine on ice with a twist
of lemon.

Cedar shingles in a red wine
reduction; the marble hearth

flickers
as the fire dies.
1972 Chevy Nova on the radio,
with a cheap blue suit in the background, humming.
Half past the torn curtains and time
for a shower.
A golden locust chirps and the revolution
begins.
Thousands.
And honeysuckle is a thing of the past.

Before It Mattered

I'd rather feel the cold slice of shale
breaking my bones,
I'd rather be an unclaimed fortune
under miles of earth,
I would rather
be a spotted pony dying of thirst,
on a battlefield of stench,

and rather than looking
through the dust of those before me,
I would
rather be
sipping blood and wine in Antioch,
with Roman heathens
fishing from the ancient lake.
I understand only the calm sound
of clicking pebbles
in my boots
as I imagine
Caesar in a robe of thorns,
with Christ standing on his neck,
rather than kneeling
in his shadow.

Chosen

A handsome fat man wearing plaid
pants and black tennis shoes
grins down at the baby.
He turns to the new father, thrusts
a cigar in his face and says
"Congratulations!" Dark spit
flies from his mouth.
The cigar hangs in the air,
his plump-finger grip, wiggling slightly.
"Who are you?"
The fat man chuckles
as only fat men can do
and taps the Plexiglass window.
"This boy here has been chosen! You hungry?"
"NO, and who the hell are you? Chosen? You need
to leave."
He stuffs the cigar in daddy's top pocket
and slowly shakes his head.
"There's always trouble. It's never a smooth transition.
Listen, let's take a walk, you and I. Outside. We'll
puff on cigars and have a nice talk,"
"SECURITY! I don't know you and you need to leave.
SECURITY!!"
The fat man folds his arms across his chest
and leans back against the wall.
"Mr. Robinson, what is it?"
"Nurse, who is this guy? I want him out of here.
He's not part of our family and he is acting very strange.
I want security to take him outta here!"
"Easy now, Mr. Robinson, which guy did you see?
Who is it?"
He sticks a finger at the wall and shouts. "HIM!!"
"Mr. Robinson, there isn't anybody there.
Come and sit down, have some coffee.
I'll get the doctor. It's been a long week,
Mr. Robinson."
"HE'S RIGHT THERE!!"
The fat man lights his cigar and waits.
"AND HE'S SMOKING!! STOP HIM!!"

"Mr. Robinson! Take it easy!!
There is nobody here but us!!
Cheryl, please call a code. Hurry, dear."
"WHAT?? Has everybody gone INSANE??"
He lunges at fat man and hits the wall.
He jumps back and sees him
in the nursery now,
behind the Plexiglass,
smiling down at the new
baby boy.
"HE'S GOING TO TAKE MY SON!!"

When the code team arrives,
three security guards restrain Mr. Robinson
with much effort.
As they lead him away, he looks back to see
the fat and handsome man
in plaid shorts and black tennis shoes
pick up his newborn baby boy by the arm
and drag him away.
He screams.
For the Chosen
one.

Pink-faced and naked, the baby lifts his head
from the grass.
"Where are we going, fat man?"
He pulls a black tie from his neck and helps
the boy to his feet.
"We are here."
They clean the stone with white
hands and the grave disappears.
"Where are the bones?" asks the man with
pensive eyes.
"You'll get used to it." said
the fat man.
"I am old, again. I have been birthed
in vain."
"You'll get used
to it."

A red-cloud breeze kills the grass at their feet.
The fat man
is gone.
A boy in a plaid shirt and
leather boots
pounds the Earth
and waits.

Everybody Dies

An intrusion is what it is, always too loud,
always speaking in a phony voice,
never looking me in the eye,
only tilting their head up to the sky
like they're pulling pure genius from the clouds.
I listen and stifle my madness for as long as I can.
So far, it has stayed inside
where nobody has to see it explode in wide,
sweeping circles of rage.
She finishes just in time, and I hear false applause,
almost like their hands are being forced together.
The man in the cheap blue suit nods to me
and I stand.
I look around, completely bewildered by their faces.
Their lips are turned up at the corners
and their top teeth are showing.
I'm pretty sure they are smiling. I move to the front
and jump over the microphone cords,
landing on the bottom step.
I stop and turn around, looking at their faces
again.
My God, they're all innocents.
They have a yellow glow about them,
cast from the poor lighting above. It makes them look ready
to die.
I hear myself talking while I hold the notebook up,
giving them some excuse as to why
I have not memorized the poems, maybe I wrote them
last night, I got too drunk, I'm nervous, on and on.
I ask the suit to turn the lights up
all the way and then I ask the yellow faces to stand.
Like beaten-down dogs,
they start to rise from their seats.
I hear myself telling a story about poetry,
about how it is better understood if you stand
and listen, some crap line like that,
and they chuckle and nod their heads and then I reach
into my belt, around my back,
and pull out the 9mm.

It wasn't supposed to be this soon but there it is,
in my hand, my finger tight on the trigger.
I tell them it is the end
and I fire first at a fat one in the 3rd row,
taking most of her forehead off at the base.
The shot has time to echo in the silence before the screaming starts
and as far as I can tell,
I fire eleven times and miss three.
I change the clip and step down into
the aisle. I pick off the ones that duck down in their seats.
Too easy. I start shooting toward
the exits and some of them turn around and run right at me.
If I can see their faces, I shoot at their eyes.
I hear sirens and head to the back of the auditorium.
Up, into the attic and out the ceiling hatch. Down
across 24th street and over a fence
into an abandoned parking lot.
I toss the gun into some weeds and head for the bar.
In a few hours I'll go to Mexico
and live until they find me.
First, I'll sip some gin
and write a poem.

Heathen

To be the first maggot
under Christ's skin
before the stone was rolled
and the lights came back on
would have
been enough
for me.

Ladies and Gentlemen

I trip over the television wires
and cuss loudly as I gather my notes.
I look slow, but feel fast and strong.
I approach the podium.
I grab the long, thin microphone
and swing it forcefully at the wooden dais.
It snaps with an amplified clatter.
The crowd makes a collective noise
that I cannot define.
I turn to them and fling my robe behind me.
I am naked!
I scream.
My poem
is still on my lips the next day,
as I struggle to eat soup in the dining room
at lunch time.

I fall

asleep.

The nurse says I have been here
for seven years.
I ask for my medication.
She gives me a pill and puts one
in her pocket.
I smile and tell her
it's okay.
I have to go.
I will be back in a few days.
She laughs and turns off
the light.

An orange spider feeds on my hand
as I drift into a black cloud.

I trip
over the television wires
and cuss loudly.

Remember

There is an unseen beauty
in the charcoal gray of a morning mist
that is so pure, this beauty,
so deeply embedded into the throat of time
that we have no choice but to keep it within us, as we would
our first morning's breath,
our last evening's blink of slow and merciful eyes
our mother's own skin, from womb to realm
and we cannot rid ourselves of it,
this beauty,
no matter the red rain at midnight
the black air at our lips
the shuddering of infants abandoned
in a ditch,
no matter, these,
for this beauty
is felt and not heard
kept and not stolen
eternal and not
tragic,
revolutionary
and not returned.

Savage

We are Blackfeet,
Gypsies of Earth; it takes
some of us longer to stretch our existence.
And to some it looks like we're standing
still.
Every so often a gang of Cree will infest
our kitchens, our
couches,
our bathrooms and garages.
We swat at them with paper war clubs
and cotton arrows.

The Hopi have tithed their crops to us
and we dynamite the percentages
with hand-held sunlight.
When we become political, the
Nazi circus reminds us that the Comanche
were first; superior
and destroyed by honor.
Finally,

as De Soto crosses into Arkansas,
we see the ghostly past
of our enemy Sioux
stretching their necks nearly 500 years
to forget.

Setting the Clock

Percocet and talk radio in a black Nova with a jammed lock,
a red light,
breathing overhead,
this is how we die.
Two dollars on the table as you claw at the trigger finger,
it is hot and a white fan sings,
this is
how we die.
Three blocks from an all night diner,
he says something in Spanish
and you wish you were in Belize,
this is how we
die.
Joni Mitchell drinking
a case of you
while the playground fills below,
this
is how
we die.
Your cat might be the only living creature that has ever really loved you,
and you begin to realize this

is how we die.

Soon Enough, For Now

It's always dark here now,
no matter the sunshine, no matter the overhead lights
that hum and buzz and whisper
in the middle of the night, when I miss
you the most.
I walk along the beach and look for you,
on the white crested waves,
look for your face in the sand,
listen for you in the song of the gulls,
wait for you near the pier, my hands
against the wet and wooden pillars,
my eyes red with despair,
my heart
my desperate heart,
I keep my unfinished longings in there
like flowers without petals,
like how we never went
to London in the Spring
or bought that stretch of land
near the hills where we met,
I kneel and I wait for light
but I know
you have taken it all with you and that is okay,
someday
I will be blinded by it
again.

Speak Not a Word

The entirety of the ocean
became mechanical, energy pushing objects
into each other; seaweed, driftwood, rocks.
All manner of debris, some of it
was strangely beautiful, most of it
was uninteresting.
I could not extract
a purpose.
The waves, the salt spray, the sand.
Energy on energy,
motion, force.
I began to say
to myself
"So what? It is mindless."
Then a gull landed softly
on a small dune in front of me.
It had pesky eyes and a ruffed neck.
It was dirty and gray on its legs
and a brilliant white
about its wings and chest.
It jammed its chipped
yellow beak into the sand beneath it,
pulled up a small clam
looked at me
and flew away
into a curtain of blue sky and sunlight.

The sum
of life's parts
is in the un-living
and the words we never think
to speak
are trapped
under the weight of the occan
at
sundown.

The Father

Nellie rolled down the gravel driveway
in a huge car that had the word "Buick" hovering
over its pale, blue hood.
Before she got out (I saw her staring into the dashboard,
biting her top lip) I turned
and went back into
the living room with the ripped green carpet and dog piss stains
that had long since turned brown.
The Father was there, so-called because of his broad
and diminutive tongue, and he held in his right hand
an old cast iron frying pan.
His left arm was missing.
I sat on the fireplace mantle
and there it was,
at my feet.
The hand was clutching a short, single-shot .22 rifle
with my name burned
into the wooden stock.
There was a stairwell between us
and he looked at me through the spindles.
I told him that if I saw him again,
I would kill him.
His left arm was no longer
missing.
He could only grit his teeth
and refused to speak.
I said again, very softly,
that I would
kill him.
After all,

he was The Father that had told me,
with great concern,
that if he had to, he would
kill me.
Over and over again
he told me this,
when I was a young boy.
I remember asking him

on those occasions
if he would spare me.
He said I had done things
I should not have done.
I offered that my sisters
were to blame.
He told me
he would kill them,
too.
So now,

as the heat of a winter fire
put sweat on my back,
I stood and moved toward him.
I saw a black swan with human hands
in front of me. I stopped.

Face down on a brown circle of piss,
my hair matted to my cheek.
The smell was comfortable
and made me feel safe.
When I turned to look again at the stairway,
he was sitting on a stair, crying,
with the .22 rifle
in his lap.
I took the gun from him
and killed him.
Soon after, Nellie came through
the screen door at the front of the house.
She was beautiful.
I told her
The Father had gone missing.
She nodded and walked away.
The fire had gone out.
The carpet and the walls
and the ceiling were made of concrete.
The dogs waited outside,
their bones shaking
in the December wind.

the essence of cassie

by chris shaw

A Summer Affair

This streak of envy, glowing green,
it surges through each aging vein.
The source of course, your mistress dear.
Her loveliness is all too clear
and drives me quite insane.

My eyes a shade of cloudy day,
flecked with a hint of wicked blue,
become a heartless, soulless pit.
I sulk into a sullen fit
when she has hooks in you.

Her streamlined body I detest,
as you caress with tender care.
You soothe and smooth with loving hand
and when I take my jealous stand,
in silent mode you stare.

All through the searing Summer heat,
how indiscreet, you do not hide.
You flaunt and taunt with no respect,
you offer only sad neglect,
while I have lost my pride.

Then when the Autumn days arrive,
you leave her. Back to me you slide
to please me, squeeze me as before.
If I had sense I'd slam the door
and leave you locked outside.

Her name is "Wind Song." How I laugh
that poetry has come to you.
You heard her sing and that's the sting,
you've never read a single thing
I've penned. I'm just your crew.

Inheritance

The beach at Maidencombe is reached
by countless steps of well-worn stone,
which open to a camber cove
of sand and shingle. On my own
I sit and contemplate the cliffs;
their curves embrace the open sea.
Old sandstone, richly-rugged red,
is topped by many a wind-blown tree.

And clinging to the craggy slopes
are patchwork flora, clumps of green.
From overhead the swooping gulls
disturb the silence. In this scene
salt water laps and agitates
the sea-weed caught in tidal flow,
while crested white, the crystal waves
fill thirsty rock pools feet below.

A hue of blues that span the sky
create a post-card, summer bright.
No hint of grey unwelcome cloud
to break the vista. Thoughts take flight
to bygone days, two hundred years
when others came across this bay.
The panorama stays unmarred
and still can thrill the heart today.

And All That Jazz

I woke this morning to the blast
of brass the bellowed through the air.
It blew the cobwebs from my brain.
My childhood home was found again.
I felt the thrill of dancing jive,
I felt my spirit come alive
to Melly, Barber, Bilk and Ball
or any other band at all

who played the jazz that we called 'trad'.
Fun skip-step taught by patient Dad
and to the thumping, stomping boom,
he'd swing me swiftly round the room.
I'd do my best with my young feet
to keep in time, to dance the beat
of trumpets, clarinets and sax
that belted out from record tracks.

Dear Mum and siblings all looked on
as Dad and firstborn daughter shone.
Small hands would clap, they'd laugh out loud
and Dad would say that he was proud
of all his children. "Form a queue,
there is a chance for all of you."
So as I write my feet can't wait,
for jazz and I have made a date.

Some Like It Hot

Sally adored the beat of heat, the sunbeams on her honeyed skin,
or running water for her bath, too hot, but still she'd step right in.
Her breakfast milk quite often boiled, too many blankets on the bed.
She sat too close to naked flames that marked her legs a blotchy red.

And how she loved the lambent tongues that licked the coals near to her toes,
then laughed and grinned as she gazed on those red-hot embers all aglow.
At times a candle she would light and place upon her windowsill,
soft flickers playing in the dark, she'd watch the waxy trickle spill.

One night while sleeping in her chair, the curtains caught the waning flame,
in silence as she soundly slept, her house flared up—she was to blame.
The blaze burned brightly through the night, consuming all things in its view,
and come the morning all was gone except a charred and blackened shoe.

With Hindsight I Regret

At noon she'd shuffle past my door, her trainers on her feet.
No need to stop and check the time as she walked down the street.
And in her hand a plastic bag, the contents were unknown.
A cigarette between her lips, her scent a cheap cologne.

Her fag-ash drooped, I'd watch amused, it never seemed to fall.
She had her own quaint style of dress, across her back a shawl.
A grand mismatch, all colours clashed, her hair unkempt and grey,
yet there was something in her mien, that's all that I can say.

She had the most determined look which focused on her walk,
so even if she said good day she didn't stop to talk.
She gave no clue from where she came or where she planned to go.
No matter what the weather was she never failed to show.

For all those years she walked my way, it was the same old route.
I fondly called her Fag-ash Lil, a name which seemed to suit.
One day she missed her exercise, perhaps she wasn't well?
A week progressed and then a month, there's not much more to tell.

Not one enquiry made by me, found her or her abode.
This may seem strange to mention now, I've missed her down our road.
We meet so many through our lives and some we may forget,
'though sadly Lil has left behind a feeling of regret.

I should have tried much harder then and offered her some tea,
but I was younger, immature and chose to leave her be.
As I've grown older I believe poor Lil was quite alone.
My mind reflects on past neglect, it's too late to atone.

In Search of Paradise

For years I've sought an answer,
in hope that I would find,
the whereabouts of paradise
if that can be defined.

I've dreamed of tropic islands,
palm beaches I adore
and 'though I've longed for sea and sun,
it seems to be much more.

I've climbed the slopes of mountains,
their peaks lace-capped in snow.
Seen crystalline clear waters,
cascade to depths below.

And mesmerized by sunsets
of gold-black-orange hue,
I've searched the whole world over
to seek the missing clue.

A man of wisdom told me,
he knows where it resides.
It is a feeling, not a place,
it's buried deep inside.

If you embrace contentment
and joy at all you hold,
then paradise is yours to keep
worth more than all earth's gold.

Going Back to My Roots

It's just as I remember, my home of long ago.
The memory lifts my spirits when I am feeling low.
I hear the Christmas knees-up, late relatives at play.
I'm sitting on the doorstep, their ghosts are back today.

All handing round their presents, the laughter and the jokes,
bright tinsel and the baubles, the dog-ends of the smokes.
Old Grandad in his braces, a pint glass in his hand,
as I eat bowls of jelly with fruit that has been canned.

And Stephen, stuffed on pork pie, my Mum will have a fit.
Aunt Alice sloshed on sherry, she's getting on a bit.
Let's do the okey-cokey, we all stand in a ring,
my Nan leads on piano, not one of them can sing.

Now in come all the neighbours, the place is tightly packed.
The booze is on the dresser, the plates of food are stacked.
The front door is wide open, we conga in the street
and everyone is happy, it is our Christmas treat.

Us young ones find the table, and hide beneath its top
and stay there telling stories until the music stops.
Then Nan comes to our rescue and we go off to bed,
there's four of us, one mattress, we snuggle head to head.

I'm unsophisticated, but don't think that's a fault,
It's something that I'm proud of—I come from earth's plain salt.

Force 10

If by chance
you care to glance,
and peep in Beth's room while she sleeps,
a hurricane has swept a path,
and littered wreckage piles up deep.
All her garments
rumpled, crumpled, stacked
upon a ransacked bed.
Wardrobe doors swing free from hinges,
loosened
when composure fled.

Empty shelving,
cleared of old books,
dumped upon the dark wood floor.
All her soft toys
in the corner,
from her schoolbag papers pour.
Half-mast curtains, lamp-shades tilted,
broken beads which look like mine.
See my long forgotten lipstick, safe
inside her pink-walled shrine.

Boots and shoes, how many are there?
East or west the pairs are tossed,
goods once classified as missing
have turned up,
they've not been lost.
In the morning, hear a whistle.
Watch the red card handed out.
She'll be clearing up this chaos,
on her face,
no doubt a pout.

treasure

in his personal effects
a wallet
well-worn brown leather
ingrained with life

she hesitated
opened and found
inside with new notes
a name-band
the one placed on her tiny wrist
minutes after her birth

he had treasured it
for thirty-nine years

she swallowed her sadness
and felt so valued
so precious.

Watch My Lips

At times we take for granted the gifts bestowed at birth.
It's not until we lose them, we understand their worth.
I bellowed as a baby, was vocal as a child,
tried cadence for seduction, screamed out when I was wild.

Last week my voice turned weary. It whispered and grew weak.
For days now I've been silent, a mouse without a squeak.
My loved ones are all smiling, believing it's dead cute
as she who's always talking, is now completely mute.

Frustrated by my prison with thoughts I can't release,
God help the ones who mock me, the ones enjoying peace.
For when I'm back to normal, I swear that they will pay,
my tongue will do some whipping and then they'll rue the day.

Benson Weir

I walk the sturdy, steel-grey bridge
that spans the river's flow,
to watch the gush and sudden rush
of water plunge below.

The wicked weir with all its force,
a source of fear to some.
And yet it holds a canvas bold
to thrill for days to come.

A thousand swirls of crystal twirls
cascade and dance with joy,
as continents of floating foam
drift round a bobbing buoy.

A surge of moving marble peaks
collide with broken reeds,
and small suds on the margins form
a line of cut glass beads.

Too soon they merge then disappear,
lost in the downstream race,
where all becomes a memory
of crystalline and lace.

Manorbier Castle

Perched high above a peaceful beach,
with stunning views across the coast.
Come visit Manorbier with me,
a castle haunted by old ghosts.
Baronial home of Norman style,
it's stood the test against fierce gales.
A treasured gem in Pembrokeshire,
much loved by Gerald, son of Wales.

The limestone masonry was built
and crafted by twelfth century hands.
Both towers, turrets round and square
look wind-worn but still proudly stand.
See strong and crenellated walls,
unspoiled by Medieval gloom.
No savage blows by evil foes,
have turned this place to silent tomb.

A quiet solitude pervades,
an ambience of years gone by.
A chapel and an old gatehouse,
the inner ward sees open sky.
On cloudless days this spread of blue
will fall to greet a sparkling sea,
and from the heights one's eyes can roam
to cast themselves on lush country.

The laid out borders edge the green
bedecked in glory, summer bloom.
Bright colours lift the whole display
to scent the air with sweet perfume.
I've stood and felt enchanted here,
looked back to times of toil and strife.
Heard strings plucked on a soulful harp
and mused on being Baron's wife.

My Amour

I rest beneath a lofty oak
with canopy of cooling shade.
I feel its light breath on my brow
while I sit curtained in the glade.

A rustle sounds of trembling leaves,
I hear the murmur of the brook
as I reflect upon my love,
and read from pages of his book.

True passion burns, a trail is left,
It carves and scars my willing heart
and I'm so lonely when he's gone,
I dread the time that we're apart.

A life of sorrow I would lead
without his presence close to me.
His name? Come nearer, I will tell.
I'll spell it out, it's P-O-E-T-R-Y

Yesu Ben

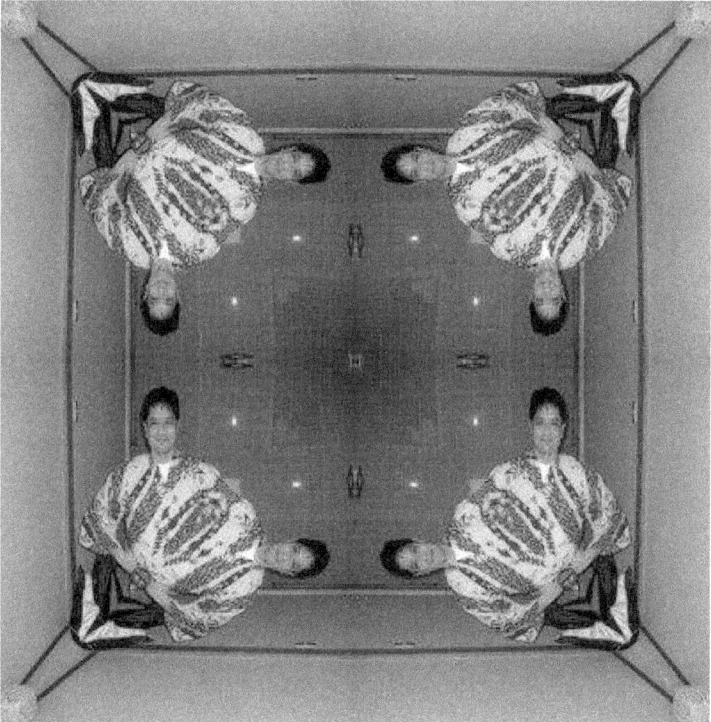

by benny de la cruz

A Transfiguration

Past midnight, when only street lights glimmer,
but glimmer only from the caddisflies
and moonlight moths mesmerized by shimmer,
one runs away by some devise
of the intelligence of his nature
and clicks away
rhyme that portrays
and defines who he is, a lovely creature…

Upon Which to Stretch Out

On an icy meadow I lie,
Ten million stars shivering,
In unison begging,
Like bees in a concerto,

To be taken into,
My embrace.

My naked faltering voice,
In night rhymes invite,
My outstretched arms,
Become like portals,

And they stream,
Filling my eyes with light.
Causing little shining tears
To well over,
To the grassy universe,
Underneath…

my head.

Disowned

It isn't all perfume and rose
a worm invades the bud
a hateful storm, cold winter throes,
or suffocating flood.
Life scorns, it mocks its own behests
And stares unsparingly; it jests.
I shadow caged
I shadow caged
In this gangrenous iron nest.

You reach for dreams, past barring threats
a wild eyed woman's pelt
You hide in closets, silhouette
from righteous Father's belt.
Infected grass and putrid crud
My cradle underneath this mud
Time disowned bridge
Time disowned bridge
Delays the freezing of my blood.

Learning

What use books, knowledge, ways to see the world,
To learn to deal with it, its laws and men,
What use to know protection and defense,
And poetry, why flags are rolled and then unfurled?
What use is it to read and write and see
The various means to help our fellow men,
To feed our children, love our friends and be
The best and use our gifts the rightest way we can?
We carry empty baskets in our heads
To fill with what's needed as we tread
For we are hungry beings, we need bread
And work and sweat and at the end of day a bed.
For once we stop this learning sweat, we age
And lose the script and role meant for this extant stage.

On HPB's The Voice of the Silence (Fragment One)

Before the sun can penetrate your veil
to make of thee a white winged angel free,
you must, Lanoo, peel off your guise, your jail
and slay your mortal lunar self and flee.

For to possess your soul, fight Self and flesh,
twins, and yet one must perforce disappear
and in the struggle, must taste pain and thresh
'til sense and person cease to interfere.

'Til snake and serpent rise above the head
and unify the Spirit and the man,
'til every drop of his blood has been shed
And he becomes himself the Path he scans,

'Til then he cannot be a god of air
for true gods don't a shroud or mantle wear.

Mercy

He was glad
And thrilled, and filled,
and best of it
Was a yearning
childlike freedom
That he had felt again.
Through torments
He had wished,
if God would just permit
a fresh new start,
To be with them once more, and right
The wrongs he did.
It'd be all that he'd ask for.
This window would renew his strength
And give him what he started with.
Plainly a gift he didn't deserve,
…A lease on life…in a place of punishment,
A few more years upon his feet,
A few more years to breathe.

When in April
(The Fair)

At long last, clouds have lifted and dispersed;
The pikes have reappeared; the land is wet;
The air smells of fresh earth; anguish reversed;
Yellow flowers dressed in green—proud and set
For a new day's longed for exchange of views,
The meadow has become a noisy place;
Flora in brightest fashion clothes and shoes;
A conversation lively, vines embrace;

On privacies and on oppressive trees,
On rain, on covert sneak of weed on ground;
they're drinking to the renaissance with glee
A cycle's been concluded; life is found!
The conscious world sings, breathes and is aware!
With tenor voice that echoes in the air!

The Empty Street Below

To a lone concealed contracted corner,
The empty street below clambers than curves
Quite gradually, it tramples by, now swerves
Before my house, yet for a while, defers.

It did defer from that dim under-shade,
I did intently compute its voyage—
Which was unhurried like a pilgrimage
Yet tempting that I joined in its parade.

It did not bore me stiff, and I did find
Its light, the one that peeped from round the bend,
The one it sought for counsel or to mend
Its faults as most of them are seekers blind,

Or perhaps yet again, for mere relief,
As howling storms—those chill and twisting streams
Did for a laugh that sounded like a scream,
Embraced this frightened region, gave it grief.

The gale's long gone and left this frugal street
Much as it found it—austere and half-lit.
The minute plants and stones that line and sit
Have stooped all low; all seemingly to greet

Or hide their indignation. They much look
Like a horde of high-hat men protesting
My vast absurdity. I laugh thinking
that monarchs feel this way as in the books.
And perchance too how their inferiors feel.
Yet I'm inclined until it re-appears—
Those faded footsteps, that each dawn draw near,
Of a peculiar gait nearly surreal.

Of times gone by, yet all the time unfazed
And slow and dawdling like he weren't among
Us faceless faces, and did not belong.
I keenly for his profile bleak did gaze,

For him to trample by, marching to mock
eternity, until this bearded man
In rags, unfeatured by the half-shown sun,
Who bore upon his back an arduous sack

Of kindles, emerged, urging me to hack
And verify my charts in haste, if I
Have indeed, by a wicked witch's eye,
To vanished ages, been transported back.

Carnation

A grassy walk, carnation-lined stone stairs
I climb to see them murder my adored.
For centuries, I've paused to smell her hair
and adulate a scent no queen has poured
Onto her palm. They've fought for one mere whiff,
one vision quick of her entrancing sway.
And having learned, her sweetness smeared as if
she's lost her drift, and earned their heartless bray.
My garden's carnations have disappeared;
The wondrous fragrances have lost their trails
and weeds of hatred overgrown have cleared
the path of rhyming flowers, rudely flailed
inducing age old Mother back to sleep
that her sweet rhymes, be thrown into the heap.

40 Days

The clayish ground has become silvery
From damp to dry as weeds turn yellow brown.
Abandoned yet adorn by glimmery
of shining bits of sand strewn all around
and remnant bones. This ship that sparkles rife
stands like fire as brilliant as midday,
as if it ruled the dunes and winds above.
No spirit, scholarly nor low of life,
whose sense is neither lost nor gone astray,
would seek out here his solitude and love.

Except for one, a foolish seeker, old
Or older than the goddesses of Time,
In tattered rags that dazzle like pure gold,
Would touch with fingers joyful and sublime
The stubbly grains of this sanctuary's earth,
This harbor for time's wearied travelers
Tired of the endless bickering and race
To reach the empty mountain tops from birth;
A race to last 'til death, and crueler
Than being tortured and spat on the face.

Yet in the midst of hell upon her earth
Shall rise the monument of her advice
Yet round her torso is the bloodied girth,
And crown of thorns to mute her many sighs:
The steps to her Golgotha, lessons learned,
The lashes on her back, benevolence.
And from her side shall drip out clemency,
As tears from both her eyes, her deep concern
For this persistent protracted weariness,
Thirsting for faith in man's humanity.

On Her Plight

A pox, a blight, a cursed end
An instance of regret
Let hope ring out—a message send
That love will pay the debt.

Let Earth continue, hands be lent
Give ease to this passage
Let faith ring out and stars assent
reconstruct the damage.

Soft

My beautiful, subtle, demure,
gentle as a rose's petal—
scent so sweet, enticing and pure,
like soft flakes of snow that settle
on leaves, fascinate me and more—
but honey please, tonight…don't snore.

Breakfast with Mom

she cannot hide her smile
it shows
in crinkles of her eyes
i tell her so
she lets it out,
a curl
and cracks a pun
catching the peal
of stainless spoon and fork
and silent sipping
of coffee,
…a lifting moment.

abandoned words

by bruce noblitt

Emerald City

Midtown sunlight arrives
Another greasy dawn
reflected on worn stainless
Tucked away in leaden mind
the alchemy of a childhood
sits unused, blocking the exit
of golden pigtails
a simple time
a first love
Alone, surrounded in a city that never
sleeps
a red-eyed future contemplates
a life as cold
as a second cup of coffee

Code Blue

Torn lace
pillow fights between
temperamental angels
drifting silent
kissing a blessing
uttering a curse
a condemnation
death sentence
look to the sky and see
inconvenience
joy
death
from where you stand in life
as the snow covers us
all

Drunk Tank

Revel in the time
of mist across the delta
fertile with the horrors
of ages not lived
but remembered
Crossing the lines
feeble attempts of
battle weary realist
making no headway
retreats
as lucid madness routs
fluid once again
carried on a river of Baccuhs
Morpheus
subdues the demons
astride the beast
until the dawn
reddens with rage
of a new day

Leathernecks

Witness
Forgotten children from Christmas past
swimming in the undercurrents
of anonymity
Blemish on the face
of society
covered by
potions of fade cream
applied by knee jerks
running too fast to read
the directions
Stand beside them at the corner
Breathe
Let them know you are alive
and pull them from
the grave

Only the Strong Survive

Iron men
Lined up
Ready to battle the beast
Growing stronger
In a man made Hell
A fiery glow
Sulphurous fume
Announcing its release
Sparks fly
engulfing the corp enlisted to
direct the
flow
Molten river of yellow heat
captured in-spite of its rage
Sitting and simmering
Awaiting the form it will take
Once again a battle one
over a dangerous formidable foe
But the beast that seals this cadre's fate
Flows from not the furnace's blast

but an unseen accountant's pen.

Paradice City

The afternoon sun
breaks through to my brain
yelling at me
like my mother
before she threw me out of her house
A dull ache tells me I'm alive
and in need of another round
loaded into the chamber
to silence my protesting liver
about being abused once again
pussy!

The stench of cheap blond
and the aftermath of lust bludgeon my nose
I look to open a window but the glass is shattered
by shoes I threw at it last night so the room can
breathe
The beast thought I slayed last night awakes
claws at my back wishing me a good morning
Who the fuck is she to tell me what kinda morning it is
we missed it now it's sliding towards magic time
she needs to leave so I can puke in peace

I wonder what's on tap downstairs
anyway it's a reason for me to get dressed
find out
and write
another chapter of life.

Elephant's Graveyard

Lonesome wind running through the halls
Finds no one at home to play
Jumps through wide open panes
Glass diamonds litter the pave
The lost Eldorado
lost its luster
alchemy turning gold to rust
A six pack of drums
toxic to the taste
brew ready to bust
A card board shack
set on the edge of oblivion
shelters a solitary soul
What's another painful memory
to erase
in the place that time forgot.

Urban Renewal

The wind blows red brick dust
along the avenue
staining the abandoned cars
watching progress
One more swing of the ball
My past crumbles
but not
my memories

Sunday Morning

A rising dawn pushes aside a neon valley
ushering out Mexican music backfilling with
Negro preachers competing for my
redemption
I would prefer static but I can't fight the Lord now
I have a headache
You smell of nicotine and swill
doesn't matter
just bring that warm six pack with you
before we turn the lights out on
today
I'll be upstairs
Don't keep me waiting

Be Silent

Leave
Don't speak
Hollow words
Reverberate
In the cold empty heart your love once warmed

Eminent Domain

Horned skeletons
covered with fly specked
leather
Dry as the mud
in the cracked river bed
The lucky rise an arm
skyward pointing the way to
salvation
Free from this manmade hell
the last act completed before
departure
with no baggage
Curse the robber dam
draining life
while sleeping
in a feather bed
far from the dust.

Low Tide

Day breaks the grey veil along the horizon
late as usual
The old man looks out a broken window
in a salt box shack
wondering to fish or cut bait once again
Crying gulls float on a fetid breeze
searching for a quick feed
In front of the shuttered cannery
Steel pilings, the color of sunset, rise from the mud flats
denuded by neglect
beg to be put to work
The man pulls the tattered rags over the window
his mind made up
to cut bait once
again

Revisionist Rattle

Slip past the chain link carefully
we have much to see
pay no mind to the hobos camping by the road
they have seen our kind before
Look, over there in the pile of bricks
camouflage to some but to the keen eye
you can see the heart of the beast
still a blaze

Look closer
see the glow of the alchemy that built
the Industrial backbone
the backbone that made America rise
to stand and fight
to call out and offer hope and shelter
to those that had none

Ah, but look harder and you will see those that the beast
call too close in order to be fed
listen on the wind that passes through the weeds
above the clanging of forges
widows and orphans
calling out to the loved ones
anguished and cursing this place
that promised a better life

See now the detritus of time
the glorious past cast aside as a pariah
by revisionist smug and safe in hindsight
sins committed by our elders
that ruined us and ours for life
just back away in horror
and shake your head at the callousness of the past
careful now
you don't want to trip and fall
over that rusting backbone
that nobody wants to claim
as their own.

little sparks

by saundra schmidt

Coping

One feels the fire light her fingers, hits the keys
while another beseeches some deity, on her knees;
still another stares despondently into nothing at all,
or watches fearfully as shadows creep along the wall.

Some think of moments when they were filled with life,
wondering how it all comes to the point of a knife.
Some pet little kittens, and feed wild birds,
no, there is no relevance to think so is absurd.

Will you try to reach out when your forces are all spent,
beg a little help out of the fast drying cement
made out of isolation, cast in a mold of fear.
I'm screaming out for help. Does anybody hear?

Wizardry of Domination

Diminishing my pride in admittedly unprofitable goals reached
Has become your latest wave of staff, your wizardry of domination.
Weakened as if from bloodletting when too much has been leeched,
You still expect my behavior to modify in accommodation
To your needs and wonts; and this you make quite clear
Is your right by hierarchy, me being way below your status.
The immaterial substance of things which I hold dear
Are paid for by my suffering, seldom in hiatus.
The sting has gone from my defensive responses;
My sarcastic whip no longer cracks a lash.
My self-image is a ghost now; what haunts is
Remembering the wishes that you smashed.

You could reanimate me if you wanted;
If I did not still love you, I would not be haunted.

This Ain't No Westside Story

Now on the Westside the new streets the new shops, good schools
are free from the blood, sweat, and piss that foul the ghetto pools
kids can still be kids there—all the girls have starry eyes
they don't know about the hunger and the government lies;
and the boys think competition means winnin' fuckin' games,
but in the 'hood they live and die and no one remembers names.

You get a free education from growing up downtown
if you'd like a demonstration we can step outside...
Watch your step—think you're safe behind that tinted glass?
You're liable to get jacked if a thug needs a ride.

Like the mangiest dogs and the most feral cats,
the gangs on the streets turned around their hats
for a reason, then someone thought it cool and made it trendy;
but the real deal ain't on Facebook and hell no, you can't 'friend' me—
I mean, look at all the shootings and the looting during riots.
We were ready then because we're criminals, we're pirates.

You get a free education from growing up downtown
if you'd like a demonstration we can step outside...
Watch your step, think you're safe behind that tinted glass?
You're liable to get jacked if a thug needs a ride.

Twenty-One Weeks

Sing me a song from long ago,
The sun hangs low; the willow weeps.
Places in dreams, forgotten, faces…
The night has fallen, the child sleeps.

Curled fetal form breathing in and out,
An infant dreams return to womb.
A chill of February wind
Rouses him too soon.

Gnarled leafless tree limbs
Sway outside the shutters,
Scratching like clawed appendages;
Leaves lie rotting in gutters.

The mother hears her child's cry
Turn desperate and needing.
She slips out of her warm blanketing,
With dreams of her youth receding.

Once held to the breast the child
Abruptly ceases crying.
Comfort comes so easily,
As does satisfying.

Another infant long ago
Was left beneath the willow;
He haunts the dreams of one
And the other cries into her pillow.

A young woman sitting on a swing:
Not swinging, simply sitting,
She hums a melancholy song,
Busy with forgetting.

The bloom of youth still is blushed
Dusk-rose on her cheeks.
Yet she has aged decades
Over the last twenty-one weeks.

She feels the chill of February wind
And slowly walks homeward.
Her daisy-chain day memories
Are left strewn in the boneyard.

Sing me a song from long ago;
The sun hangs low, the willow weeps.
Erase the dreams of what might have been…
The night has fallen; the secret keeps.

Dirt Road Poetry

Wheels are turning, gears are greased.
I put down my foot so the speed will increase
And the brakes are failing like it or not...
I'm really revved up, yes my engine is hot!

The highway of verse is crowded with billings,
Do this and try that and the words are all spilling
Out of the fuel tanks of wanna-be writers
Who hug the curves in the road ever tighter.

As limos and hummers and hybrids and classics
Go cruising through the rush hour traffic
Of poem after poem and the mileage used
Has the route to the true destination confused.

Burnout and roll off down some strange road of dirt,
Because poems just don't count much if they don't hurt.

Unsafe Waters

The little things that seem so very trite
Can rise up from the unconscious, a great white,
Razor sharp teeth, jaws clamp down and lock;
This happens every time "we need to talk..."

Too many times I let what irks me go,
For I will lose any argument. You know
The right things to say to appeal to reason.
I steer clear of those waters, in shark season.

Sail away then, Captain, leave this bay
Whose source is all the tears I washed away.
Soon the lands will flood with those I'll shed
For the last hope to be loved I had is dead.

I will never fathom your depths, though I sink.
Is the shadow coming closer what I think?

Home, to the Sea

A siren's song, a silver cross
A reckoning beneath churning seas;
A wind that ripped the fronds from trees.
A wail and screech of loss.

A vicious rain that filled the ship,
Broke down the towering crests.
Sea-girl held sailor to her breast,
Kissed his cold blue lips.

His open glazed eyes saw not
Her own eyes pale and green;
She saw things that he had seen,
Read his final dying thought:

From this flesh, finally free;
Ah, the sea, she cradles me!

Rising

Tight-wire walks and flying trapeze acts,
Triple-axle spins, pirouettes and swan-dives;
Human pyramids that tower all the way to heaven,
Where I topped then fell, back down into nothing.

Marathon races, swift lightning bolt sprints,
Juggling, mind-boggling, even spoon-bending will;
The body sings electric signaling impossible
Seeming into being, streaming ultra-essence

Aria and tenor near beyond frequency to hear,
Mathematical equations that stretch the mind full width;
I dream with greater power than explicable by wit,
And elevate the rising of potential even higher.

Spazmatic Serenade

Epileptic dancer,
Chaos is playing our song;
Strobe lights
Ensure seizures…
Lit up limbs thrash,
Lashed by lasers…
Rave on
Oh my dearly demented,
The air is overwhelming me,
Scented
With the acrid alarm
Of short-circuit.

Tempo quickening,
The macabre grace
In contortions
Is like a puppet
Pulled by ninety strings,
Techno drumbeat
Throb and pulse
Hypnotic
Then in fluid motion
He goes limp,
The finale: (applause)

The critics
Called the performance
Grand Mal.

Matchmaker

I saw the dawning 'tween the two;
I watched the sunset after dusk;
I heard the lamenting of each—
Kept quiet in my trust.
The maker of peace that I was born to be
Yearned to give a push;
The diplomat that I trained of myself
Came forward to say, "Hush,
These things will be if meant to be,
In whatever way they will."
I am glad to see the two find
A new sunrise, and a destiny to fulfill.

Harm Done

The Nevada desert has become ash;
It turns the rain water black in the wash,
Drains in the lake and kills all the fish,
They float to the shores and rot in the brush.

Monsoons were absent for the last few years;
An ominous cloud looms over, then pours
In colossal sheets and obscures the stars,
Filling the streets and dousing the fires.

Nature, it seems, would reclaim this sere land,
Waving, in circles, her furious wand.
I watch the blue bolts of lightning ascend
Counting the miles by thunderous sound.

How can we make up for what we have done,
Now that the time for forgiveness is gone?

Rethinking the American Dream

In my country, not having a television
is a sign of abject poverty.
Not having electricity is unthinkable.
Not having a home? Criminal vagrancy.
I am not as bad off as that, but close enough
to know that in some places
the slight roundness in my cheeks
would be a sign of prosperity.
I can spare some change now and then,
buy someone a hamburger and fries;
but I can't change the fact
that there are fewer and fewer opportunities
or that the middle class rut
is the best I hope to be stuck in
continually seeking a way out from under
approaching tyranny.
I don't vote anymore;
I don't believe in anybody
and if the amassed impoverished
ever rise up together
they will probably be eradicated permanently.
Oh, give me some green land
with fertile soil, some cattle and sheep,
some seeds and a few tools,
a clean water source,
and watch me thrive
happily.

Decompress

I am at my best when those in dire straits
reach out for my help like my existence relates
to everyone whom I have connected to; contemplate,
if you will, how that changes my whole attitude.
Yes, perhaps I've helped others but it is my debt of gratitude
that I owe to them, my peers, poet-friends, my best hope
to create a serene future where not only can I cope
with my own post traumatic circumstances, climb the slope,
but also stand atop the peaks with those whom I have met
in a place where understanding and empathy dissolve regret
into a watered down concoction, not a poison like before;
oh, if I might change the world by words that reassure
and turn guilty feelings into wisdom, worked hard for,
I have been successful and I can at last find peace.
Bring me your pressurized emotions, together we will find release.

spilled milk

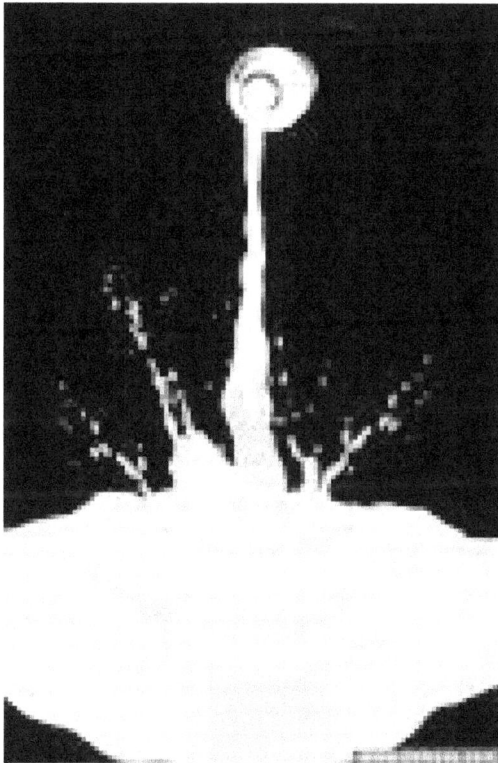

by **brian s. mayo**

Muskrat

If you ask
a muskrat
about his day
you will be
amazed
at what you learn
in the silence.
Then
he will bite you.
If you ask
a weasel
to solve complex equations,
he will go mad.
Then he
will bite you.
If you give a banana
to a monkey
he will smile politely—
and make plans
to rip your face off.

You

You smile,
I beam.

You laugh,
I am amazed.

You wink,
…and the barn
burns

Pinto

I don't remember the year
but I was driving a Pinto when I last saw her.

She was wearing faded Levi's,
and her hair——a tangled mess of promises.
The promise of summers at the cottage
with blue umbrellas and a catfish trapped in a tiny boat
and unexploded firecrackers on the beach
the morning after the 4th.
And barefoot!
She was a natural in the sand.

We hugged,
and drove off in opposite directions.
To what?
To a half-empty closet.

I couldn't possibly use the hanger
she left on the floor.

Unknown

Like a frozen pond
opaque
unknown
until this very minute

she, too, was hiding among tall pines

you scrape
with a gloved hand
needing something
anything
you scrape and brush
exposing
thick, heavy ice

only dark, frosty windows
with feathery edges
of the coldest
white.

Workhorse

"It's loud."
The water was two hundred feet below,
down a steep, sandy slope.
We could hear the waves riding in—
breaking apart on the beach
in a strange, random rhythm—hypnotic.
It was minutes from full-dark.
The day had been cold and cloudy, but a low sliver of moon
promised clearing skies.
A light but steady wind slipped through tall patches
of dune-grass, keeping the bugs away
and making our small fire dance.
We sat on the sand and
huddled under a single blanket.
An enormous driftwood log gave support to our backs.
I wondered if some poor work-horse
was forced to drag it up the hill
a hundred years ago.
I pictured him getting whipped and screamed at.
We sipped hot coffee, and enjoyed our buzz
while staring out over the void.
I imagined shipwrecks and the deep, dark cold.
The weight of her head against my shoulder felt just right.
The stars appeared all at once—spilling
from a horrible cloth sack.
She put her hand on my leg and
my pulse quickened.
"Let's go swimming in the morning…"

I thought it was the greatest idea I'd ever heard.

Schrödinger's Cat

This is the exact spot where
Meyer vanished…
He was wearing a Guayabera shirt, which
seemed out of character.
We were debating Schrödinger's cat.
He was standing
right there
on the sidewalk.
He glanced at his watch.

I bent down to tie my shoe,
when I looked up—
he was gone.

I sometimes wonder
if he is alive
or dead
or, like the cat,
somewhere in between.

Five More Minutes

I am hoping for five more minutes.

Five minutes
to remember the smell of the sea.
Five minutes to recall
the rustling glory of tall corn.
Five minutes
to mourn a dying pine
on a wind-swept
dune.

I need time to
look under the lily-pads,
cut open the belly of a snake,
see God reflected
in a horse's eye.

Give me five more minutes
to call a friend.
dash off a few apologies.
have another cigarette.
write the last chapter—
have the last laugh.

Five minutes to look beyond
the thicket.
Five minutes to gather a few
smooth stones.
Five minutes to take out the garbage.
Five more minutes, please…

because
I wasn't ready.

Band-Aid

I found
the band-aid
from the tip
of your little
finger
curled on the rug
this morning.
I can't
bring myself to
throw
it out,
so I
stuck it
in the hollow
turtle
on my windowsill.

I briefly
consider the DNA
that surely resides
within,
but, not being
a mad-scientist
with access to
a state-of-the-art
cloning facility,
I fail
to
see
what
good
it
will do
me.
I have decided to keep your coffee-maker.

Quick-Fixes

You hoped it would save you
this thing
plucked from dead and rotting
giants.
You hammered and shaped it
into
what you needed,
what you needed
to keep
from going the way of saints
and suicide-bombers.

but it wasn't even close
to perfect
and, after a while,
after too many feathers
on the forest floor
you stopped believing,
believing
in miracles and magic dogs.

So you looked inside and
underneath.
You studied dewdrops.
You pondered donuts and
dark-matter.
And you built a little trick box.

In it goes ONLY
the truth
(as you see it).
The truth:
pasted from scraps of torn paper
and plastic bags.
The truth:
pulled from dinosaurs
and the bellies of dead pelicans.
The truth:
discovered on the back of
toads and fine timepieces.

The truth about
quick-fixes
and killing-floors.

And, after a time…
you begin to write, again
and you allow yourself a tear.

Not Alone

They say Indians walked along this creek
and I believe it.

This trail is littered with winter's wreckage.
I choose my steps carefully—my moccasins
printing decayed leaves into the loam with
barely a whisper.
I sense ancient souls here among the trees.
Weathered Oak and Elm
giants, twisting upward, seeking light,
but today—a dismal
gray wash
filtered
through a witch's tangle of
creaking bone and gnarled claw.

The hollow beat of a distant woodpecker, then
a deep stillness. Fresh deer tracks
pepper a muddy slope to the water, gleaming
darkly through a growth of saplings.
I spot a familiar rock, a jagged recluse
jutting from a pebbly shallows.

It gets quiet as dusk nears.
I pause, holding my breath.
I leave the path
and vanish beneath
waiting pines.
A purple mist descends…

I am not
alone.

Spilled Milk

I don't want to hear about
your garden
or what you had for dinner
or
how much you love
the rain.
Don't show me
another mountain
or tell me about
your dreams.
I've had more than enough
sunlight and stained glass.

I want to know how you felt
Christmas morning,
when your dad
kicked the dog so hard he
broke two of its
ribs.
Tell me about the lady next-door who
backed over her cat, after
asking if the coast was clear,
and how she looked at you accusingly
as it lay squirming on
the driveway.

Show me the nine-year old boy
who did a lousy job
sweeping the garage
and got yanked out of bed
at three in the morning
on a school night to
do it right
this time.
Let me see him
hiding in his bedroom closet while
his mother runs
to the neighbor in her nightgown
and the dog

is being drowned in the family pool.
Tell me about the uneasy glances,
when your dad suddenly reached for the salt,
and you flinched so hard
you spilled your milk all over the table.

Tell me about the good times

Shotgun

It runs around in
your head
like
a starving mouse, driving
you mad.
Sometimes, you feel it
scratching
on your skull;
little claws
carving tiny furrows
in bone.

It wants out,
and
you know it will
get out,
even if it has to eat
your damn brains—and
when it does,

it's going
to turn a shotgun
on the world.

Hummingbird

It's not something you can hold
in your hand
like road gravel
or an umbrella.
It can't be measured or
quantified
or put in a Styrofoam cup
or slapped
on the end of a smooth stick.
This feeling, this fleeting
departure
this paradise
this promise
has hummingbird wings
and only I
can see it
feel it
feel its tiny heartbeat
hear it
flutter past my ear
and sometimes
when the sun is below the pines
if I am very still
a dream will settle on my shoulder
and within my chest
dawn breaks
on a wide, sparkling stream
where the dragonflies
race
and the Brown Trout
leaps
and is almost never caught
in the jaws
of a bear.

the poetry of

danté camerlengo

A Mourning Walk

I wake up; drink a large cup of heartburn.
I scrape last night's suicides from my teeth.
I put on my black fedora and turn
Out the door, wearing it like the night's sheath.

I only wear it when I'm abhorred,
(Like there's some other emotional way).
I step onto the sidewalk of hatred
And head into…just another cold day.

I walk not under, but around the lights
As I head down the street to meet my fate.
I see her and I know; it feels so right.
I decide to stop—after it's too late.

By the time the Sun rises I've been thrilled.
My heart is pounding, but my hands are cramped.
I never feel regret—for those I've killed—
They should have lived…closer to a street lamp.

A Night Out

Hardly ever enough is when we go,
(*This place is nice. Wonder if that piano was always here.*)
Money is not usually the issue,
(*It looks as old as the house. This really used to be a doctor's office?*)
I'm too busy being bored.
(*I like what they've done with the place.*)
We sit pretending to be a regular part of the dinner crowd,
(*I wonder what's in the attic, or the basement.*)
Waving to the people we know;
(*I bet there's an old wine cellar.*)
They drive by; see us together on the front terrace.
(*Wow! Look at these prices, is that this month's lease?*)
I get a huge chunk of cow and a house beer,
(*I'm only doing this for her. I should have dressed nicer.*)
She orders what it used to eat.
(*This taste like moon-shined rice, I'll just recommend the prime rib.*)
She tips large, feeling sorry that we've troubled the poor girl.
(*Look at her, she's so sweet. She really is beautiful.*)
I get our coats—give the guy a buck.
(*Wonder if he went through my pockets.*)
I help her into her coat; she kisses me on the cheek.
(*She really is beautiful. I should say something.*)

Danté and the Leak

Drip...
Drip...
The dull drool...
That drowns out the day,
A *dacapo* of the dampness
That dances...like a dart—
To the dale of decay.

Lich,
Lich,
Lifeless limb...
Lackadaisically lies,
A lachrymose of the languid
That laughs...darting loose—
To the lake's *Lorelei*.

The Epic Story of a Troubled, Refugee Teen's Tormented Soul, and an Epiphany of an Old Man

He went off to die
At an early age;
It took a lifetime
Of unlived days.

Darkness (not Byron's) a Luc-Bat

The deep darkness did fall.
Finally slumber stalled no more.
Thoughts arose from their core
Like ash above, they soared then died.
My voice unheard, I cried.
And then again I tried, but nay;
The words, I need to say,
Powerless on their way, took flight
Towards strange, distant light,
Then echoed back a nighttime Hell;
Inward my soul then swelled.
Tolling of Iron bells then rang.
Then a darker night came
With: thunder, wind, and rain that cuts
Large chasms out of ruts,
Valleys, canyons, your guts—a hole
Blacker than void and null;
A contrast of Sun's golden air
Life no longer needs care.
The end is now, not near or far.
Remember where we are—
As always for a star…night shines,
And awakens the mind;
It is then…that it's time…life crawls.

Green Tuque on the Corner

The hurdy-gurdy man never cared
about his monkey,
He worked the crank regardless,
and only the blisters on his sole
kept his write arm moving.

A song and dance man—who worked
for just a glance, and the chance
that we would see…some beauty
from misery—that loved
entertaining the street
people.

But he got busted for vagrancy
indecency (and some other—
religiously—probably), and
now the concrete has only
old gum and misplaced
trash on the corner.

The Provider

I shot the doe-eyed prom queen
right between the eyes, and
ate her
venison flesh.
I've killed many a cute little bunny
and wore the musk gland of a mink
for months. I've kicked
stubborn 'possums
to death with steel-
toed boots.
I trapped rats with hands
frozen and sold
their hides, and I
was always given
hominy as a side.

I hate Hominy.

He Sits on the Porch

One sits on the porch,
That faces the North,
And never feels the sun.

*The other one leaves The Flamingo
with Them,
but he won't be making it back.*

One glares at the neighbors
And reaps their benefit,
Laughs at their labors—
And how he'd've been done with It.

*Couple of blocks up 3rd St.,
they melt down
and shoot up*

"I don't feel a pulse," said the mother of three.

"That's 'cause you're not a Nurse," replied the driver.

"But…he looks funny."

"We all look funny; everybody funny—you funny too," slurred the punk.

The transparent Thalo
Of Green and Blue
Contrasted.
By a dash of Crimson
Didn't add much to cheer up the clouds
Sadness,
And he sat
Looking, Hating;
Though, he was that age once.

*They lean his limp body
between the trash
and the wall,
then cower off*

The first one
Sits on the porch,
That faces the North,
And never feels the sun.

"Where in the hell is that boy?"

Sponge

I have always known,
Yet it is just now that I am
Realizing
That I am not a very well
Educated man;
I wonder the brain—
Is it like a sponge?
Very absorbent
When young,
Constantly staying damp,
Never truly saturated
Unless completely
Submerged in thought
—liquid of all that is all—
It is full.
That is never the case.
Mind, my sponge,
My two sided, cleaning utensil:
One side rough
For stubborn stains
The other…
Abused and wrung out creature of the sea,
Everyday soaking
Up something new,
To be wrung out again.
The outer surface
Drying fast,
The inner
Damp, warm
Beginning a whole new culture
Of thought!

The Cancer

I can feel the Cancer
Spreading its tentacles
Like a billion blind squids
Eating upon the flesh,
Relentlessly,
Shitting cysts of steel
And concrete turds.
Weather-beaten, black vein
Crosses over the body
Like a tattered fishnet.

The hunger for longevity
Gives it an insatiable life.
The seizures are invasive
Procedures, that never send
It into remission.

Our end will be

Her only cure.

The Mantle Goes Down

The sun ain't up
It shines pink and indigo
It was red and orange
Just a half hour ago
But now it's fading to peach
Or maybe navy
Lighter in spots
Where the clouds are not
Green is the crest
And in days recent
This one's the best
Tonight I will faint
Tomorrow I'll paint
Tomorrow's break of day
I'll color more words I say
But right now it's definitely…
Navy
Or could you call it black
It's hard to tell
With the lights in the back
A lamp post here
An airplane there
Other than that
It's pure black
Except for the green
and gun metal gray
It's damn near
Another day
And now the night
Has grown quiet
The stars have come out
To play about
As I count
Their endless number
And slip into
My slumber.

The Saga of Earth, Wind, and Fire

The backwash from the Mother's regrets causes the oceans,
Wave after lonely wave of her tears;
The Earth grabs for her children.
Her emotional outburst sends the Wind,
With *Him* the stench of salt and rotting,
Be it flesh, or fish, or fowl, and…
Any and all sanctuaries are roared away
As the Father parries back in anger
With the dreadful heat of his perspicacity!
The Wind can no longer suffer to observe
The dissension between the two
And takes leave from his heavenly preserve.
Steps foot into the warm grains of sand
Walks across them as a messiah;
He comes to receive the wet kisses
From his Mother upon his feet;
The deep calms as he continues towards his Father.
Half-submerged, completely absorbed
His head arched back—his arms spread
Wider than he is tall, the flesh burns from his ribs.
The perspective becomes nonexistent, for the sky
Is as blue as the waters where they meet.
With eyes closed he sees only the orange
Yellow and reds of his Father's ire;
The Wind devours all that he can, and then bends
His trunk into the cooling reservoir
Of his Nurse's bosom; He stands erect
Then turns his back on his Father as he walks
Towards the jaded land, now naïve;
If he could only take flight would he be able
To love him
As much as the Lady caressing his feet.

The Truth is There

Look man…,
The truth is there, under the rug
with the crumbs and the hair
of the dog.
I don't want to see it, so I swept it there
and there
is where it'll stay
until another encore of Spring—
when I beat it out with a stick.

But I'll leave the windows open
all Summer; it'll be back,
eventually, covering everything.
And sometime next Fall,
before people stop in,
I'll put it back under there;
spend the Winter sweepin'
up theirs.

visions from
a natural heart

by frederic parker

Love

A silhouette I saw in the far blue
Your lingered scent lay softly on the wind
A morning rose slowly behind you
I thank Almighty God for you again
With finger tips and gentle hands a wish;
to build a world within a world that's shown
And give your lips a long and tender kiss
That lays between our hearts a golden throne
For love will carry us to graying years
Our love feasts on the purest hearts that grow
A peaceful day in flight beyond the tears
While soaring high I see my love below

Do promise as I lay in still repose
Upon my casket, orchids with a rose.

Last Victory at My Tomb

A blackened storm I face while it still blows
With iron will stand fiercely with shattered sword
Never bow down to opposing winds that show
Alone, I'll fight as death comes towards
A moment's calm has flown between the fight
Fear flies high before a gathering storm
Leaves me naked with a sense of right
Beyond my dreams and nightmares as they form
My enemy's glee slowed his pace 'til dawn
Arrives too late to bring my bloody doom
And finds with anger I have gently gone
Left my final breath on this deadly tomb

With bloodless edge now raised to curse my name
Falls on his sword, his lateness was to blame.

Sacred Ground

Love's flown in heart felt clouds with beating wings
Heard whispered voices which turn to gentle sighs
And kissed each pulse its heart could ever sing
Like soft feathered breaths from a butterfly
Beating hearts float across their frozen mounds
And spread thick fog as falling dew from leaves
To caress once frozen heart's fertile ground
Release its warmth so seeds begin to weave
Flourishing to heights sweeter blossoms bring
With ambition to reach the farthest sky
And now feel growing flight of tender wings
To spread upon love's wind and never cry

If love's beauty like this is ever found
It will melt with joy a heart's sacred ground

As the Light Fades

As doves flutter, dying words whisper
Silence remains haunting and Angels sing
A lone filtering ray of soft glister
To cast a fleeting shadow from doves wings
An arrowed light now pierces the dusk gray
On bended knee I pray for you with love
And touch the cold ground where your casket lays
To seek unanswered questions from above
No reason I have found for your last breath
Forgive me, As I drink this bitter wine
Release me, From the vow place in my chest
From the spirit of your shadow confined

This drop, The last from the poison I've made
Brings dark, A cold silent dark as cold light fades

Poems Along the Road

A longing ghost enticed my mind
And brushed a painting that I'd find
On her face which haunts me so
And there it dwells while fading slow

Among the ruins where shadows play
Are illusions that try to stay
They cross the bridge from other times
To echo sounds from broken rhymes

They leave their poems to be found
Along the road to ancient grounds
With hopes they're opened by a hand
Before they sink in shifting sand

The Queen's Ball

Standing in awe of nature's Queen
As she lets drop her nightly shawl
To lift her lamp beyond the clouds
And light the morning's sky grand hall

I take a seat between two worlds
As she brings forth her earthly winds;
to release the clouds I might find
A gift, as her light washes in

Rendering clouds become her dress
As she clamors for the day's ball
She is the light and the Princess;
before she puts back on her shawl

Passing Days with Sam

The end of day hits my window sill
Complete with rays from the red setting sun
That cause long shadows from an old oak tree;
to be painted on my shirt, fine-spun

The night slowly creeps in, at its own pace
Our window open, feeling a cool breeze
My dog Sam and I rest in cabin's space
Sam with his bone, me with my cut Jack Cheese

Been calm today with us just sitting here
Waiting for the passing of another day
Through our window saw a passing deer
Poor Sam barked once, deer had nothing to say

Night will fall and each star may brightly shine
It depends on cold prevailing north winds
If it blows, fog will cover the coastline
Will keep all the lobster boats locked in

I may fall asleep just sitting right here
With Sam who is my companion and friend
May awake in the cool morning, that's clear
Still sitting here, something I'd recommend.

Scottish Wars

Crashing waves a thunderous sound
Ghost ships in the background
Men on the ridge overlooking
Pipes play soft spirit bound

Lightning strikes with tremendous crack
As fog rolls in the bay
Ships have funeral pyres in racks;
to sea dead sail away

The pipes play and flutes are haunting
Men's sacrifices endure
Songs will be sung and stories told
All through the Scottish shores

Flames will rise through the unchained fog
Men's souls will fly away;
to seek the land of Scottish Gods
Women will cry this day

The war has ended flowing tears
Wives who gave flames of oars
Gifts will sustain for many years
All through the Scottish shores

Tender Kisses

A lush moon rose over a gentle face
As passion's eyes slowly lifted to smile
Small flutters, as my heart started to race
Brought sensitive lips closer for a while
How soft the moment, still touching, sublime
A winged freedom shared while bonding warm hearts
Give red feathered emotions worlds to find
Placing us in space, where joy imparts
Never mind lost time as we fly through it
Just know each kiss becomes even lighter
We'll fall back to earth while you're still moonlit
Its rays caress your face even brighter

How long the moment when shared with a kiss
It may last forever, an earthly bliss.

Cities of Gulls

Our cities now churn like seas full of gulls
Where need for food the unchained cracked door
And rage is the mask worn by every skull
Now fighting for scraps thrown on concrete floors

Beyond falling buildings where streets collide
As old garbage still decay in bird's sight
And nothing changes with death's coming tides;
to disturb rage born by sick cities blight

Children play where window glass stay shattered
And homeless men snore on each darkened street
Among the gulls and those who lay battered
Where life is lifeless and cold defeats

Far from cities rubble and worn down skulls
Live men of oath, throwing scraps to gulls.

Passion's Concerto

With wondrous eyes in a darker hue
Do you not see the setting sun shine
Behind mountain tops high in the blue
And see each cloud as they try to hide
Beyond meadows humming birds slow flight;
to gaze on beauty as you pass by
As each day completes and turns to night
Each star shines with a deeper sigh, to;
Hide their eyes from being blinded by you.

The Gift

I washed beaten up to your island shores
Battered by life's waves, breathing stopping soon
You gave me life with a care never asked
Showed me love's faith in your sheltered lagoon

I had nothing, nothing but love to share
No diamonds bright, rubies red, just my heart
To you I give to nourish and explore
With my gift a promise, we'll never part

My gift though humble, forever in your hands
I place it well without reserve or fear
On your heart's altar, on bended knee
And ask only, you keep it well my dear

Thirteen Steps

Allow me to walk thirteen steps in peace
As you leave, look back show me no sorrow
For these wood gallows will now take my life
Innocence cares not, for my tomorrows

A final kiss, my hands growing colder
Forgive them each day winds caress your skin
And think of me warmly as you grow older
Show no tears as I will see you again

Let me say, until and never forget
That I may leave you now without any fear
Having tasted your kiss for the last time
Know I will always be with you dear

Up each step I'll hear the sound of your heart
I will whisper I love you, and then depart.

a poet's trust

by elizabeth george

Empower Me

Be thirsty
and bring enough to spill…

You released
as I agreed to swallow
and with hunger gently breathed
the steam
rising against red cheeks.
Rage ensues as you comprehend
the power you have given me
once again
This contradiction whips you back to
winter when a slow
white death tightly gripped your skin
breathing in
the scent sends me there;

I have arrived
Alone
this time

A Room Without A View

today is blackened
refusing
to let the sun awaken you.
yet your favorite day is
in the hope of
tomorrow.
no one
knows this home better than I
it has too many walls.
my hearts hang on a peg
one of glass
the others
red.
the lawn is fine to roll,
but will you?
or hold everyone inside,
so you may write
poems for each.
is that your way
to say you love?
keep them captive in this room
instead of rolling with them in the grass
deciding
to imprison them too…
I wait
in the sun now
for you to come out
and play.
embrace this moment
before
tomorrow
destroys today.

For Duncan

Placed here with me
virtually…
I watched your gardens
grow beautiful
listened to the joy
of your bounty
heard the Love
of your wife and family
tasted your wine often
robust sweet smelling
with soul
you disarmed me
with your wit
the only one who could
take what I said and
make it fit
I heard your voice
felt the pleasure
surrounding you
…please know I care
my mind will be there.
a mighty sword you carry
sensuous man
with grace
take with you our hearts then
place them with Rosie
while she waits.

I Heard...

voices started missing their cue
incomplete lines blurred
to ruffle feathered
mistakes.
you took
and heated weathered sorrow
you shook
a built foundation
yet walls refused
to crumble.
furious
you stammered
I have...I have...I
have never, ever
lied to you,
I have,
have lied
for me.
hearts were left speaking
of when mistaken Love was curious,
and how one,
was just too...too damned.
the other
too damned big
to hold.
a memory lags
of how every untruth
was mistaken for a whisper
softly stroking
feathering
my skin.

Don't Even Blink

that guy
on first base
better be on my team
I know
what you're saying…
to you it doesn't matter
who they've been
or
their average as batter
but
when they talk to me
outside the pen
I want to know
I have a real
live friend,
see,
I am the pitcher
I have to be keen
this is my life
when it's here on the green
that guy on first
can't lose eye contact
'cause the ball
will be coming fast…so
if they happen to be lying
and looking at the ground
it will whip right through them
split them in half

it will whip right through them
split them
in half.

Snake Bait

for your sake, I hope you
are one of them.
for their sake, I hope
you are not.
as small sharp teeth
are dangerous to sheep
and wolves have no feelings
for the weak
to feed
to take
what they believe
they deserve.
swallow without chewing
it will hurt them less
and while you digest
they may get
the last chance to claw through
your fat fucking belly
grown
from eating
sheep.

Solitude

beauty is breathing
breathtaking
I wake to the beat of nature
thank God once again
my life shattered
still take it in
filling my soul alone again
I'd love for you
to see this stretch
toward the pleasure it gives me
but we sit in broken homes
and toil with memories
instead of grasping
the now
gasping for someone to see
them with me
knowing we all do
my enthusiasm goes unheard
as it would be absurd to scream
to strangers
yell of the feelings alike
to share
my lungs filled to capacity
can you believe the audacity of her?
interrupting my soured spirit
to walk alone within the world
I see as mesmerizing
and not to share seems
to make the feeling redundant

Two Faced

choice is needed
unwanted but vital…
letting chance turn the trick
you anticipate its approach
with no panic
your wishes immune
from all blame
The coin is chosen by fate
And with a flick of my finger
two faces spin head over head
releasing its force
its dread
confusing the gambler
now aware of no tail
between its legs
the faces leer
knowing your shock
that chance conspired
to rig the game
your options
denied
without credit or blame
prevented
as the faces
maniacally laugh
at your shame
the coin with two
smiles…paused
in mid air
then dropped
to the concrete
like lead

Termites

Waking to blue skies
I glimpse the pattern
scratched
deep within strong arms
that hold me
torn…
a finger nail
traces an outline
around my lips.
I chance a smile
remembering the tumble
through stones
crevices
now worn smooth
by tears
rough edges rounded
corners collapsed by truth
as my legs unfold
touch the floor
feeling the vibrations
your voice left behind
forever awake
talking…
I smile once more
accepting the echo of my solitary voice.

The Sociopath

the world within a mind
mistaken for reality
the fantasies become truth
as the lies get stuck on repeat
repeat the mistakes
the past sullied,
armed with no arms
flailing, falling, further faster
frightened trying to remain
history remembered
threats re-threaded…
only one name remains the same
the one
on the path who
tossed the others
off the cliff
walks on without the gift
the Lord shakes his head
knowing all the lies
that have been said
to save the ass of the fool
on the wrong path
being led
by the malignancy
in their head.

Inhabit

Like an angel whose wings have been torn
pulled to be someone she is not
over time deceived with loss
even her true color is tarnished now
by showing her despair.

The hands that could push were very precious
showing how much she cared
left too late to catch the already fallen,
she was meant to save, to love.

If she stops loving, caring
she will surely die with no worry
of where it comes.

She is awaiting a breath, a simple wisp of air
no matter now,

it will arrive

on a brisk breeze.

Keepsakes

I keep
the smile I saw when he danced
…that's all I have left
it lit his face
removed all lines
shone the brightest, yet
I keep a note
it says
To my Father
Thank you for
the greatest gift
you ever gave me…My sister
I keep dried silver dollars
the seeds still inside
That were never
to be planted…
over my Mother's eyes
I have tears
around my neck
held in golden glass
that is the wonder
of my son's heart
more present than the past
I see a soul and spirit still
wrapped in rainbow tissue paper
the sun warming their bodies
curious eyes peeking
from tilted heads
I have memories
of holding still,
waiting
for my arms
to fold around them

Breached Trust

Tears…
only tears now.
Place your hand near my heart
feel it
slow.
Rest your head on my shoulder
bones
protrude
against the real soul
moments before,
softness…
open our belief
an exit to the south, an adventure now bricked
over
safe from arms that can hurt.
Once held close, my spirit
is all that we know, all that we have reached
sensing untruth
quietly asking
why was I not enough?
Collapse is inevitable as we now unfold
trapped within
ourselves
suggesting a cocoon,
and I do,
allowing what should be
to be
begging nightfall to take us
allowing love its freedom.
In your hands,
death
was me.
Truth…
now releases
from its cold grasp
breaking free
rising to soar through
dark clouds
where new winds
find me able
to dream.

lost among the thorns

by happy hiram

The Saddest Poem Ever

A heart never broken,
The truth never spoken,
Life wrapped up like a
The poem never writt

The Volunteer

I wanted to do some good for the world
now that I wasn't homeless anymore
So I went to a workshop on AIDS volunteering.
It was some young nurses, a few senior citizens
some "opera fans" and me.

Bobby spoke about being a recovering addict
about having survived with AIDS 14 months
about going out to housing projects
and handing out condoms and bleach bottles.

He said they were reaching out to those at risk,
telling other junkies how to clean their works.
I looked around the room and thought
who is he talking to and realized it was me.

Nobody else there was going to hand out bleach
on a corner in Bellingham Square at night
So I signed up for it, what the hey
and I went to the meeting the following day.

There were 20 addicts, clean and dying
who had problems I could barely fathom
but they took the time to get to know me
to help me, to get me clean and sober.

We didn't all have so many adventures
their life expectancy was 18 months
but I owe those folks my sobriety
my happiness and even my life

The homeless, sick, addicted or dying
often have more to give than anyone
don't limit your teachers to those whose path
leads where you think you want to go.

I was a volunteer, trying to help
but I got more help than I could have imagined
now I trudge the "road of happy destiny"
looking under rocks for my new teachers.

The Ragged Boy

The pet parade was on that day
the park was boisterous and sunny
the laundry basket dirty and clean mixed
was not as bright and funny
somewhere in the dark depths
a pair of corduroy shorts
a dirty tee will have to do
I ran to the basketball courts.
The dogs and cats set on display
were not to be the show
the torn bottom of my ragged shorts
were the talk, though I didn't know
One kid grabbed a thread and soon
the shorts became a skirt
and underneath those wayward flaps
my underwear were worse
I ran home fast as I had come out
but the mob seemed even faster
lifting up my flap of shorts
and deaf'ning me with laughter.
I crawled into the old hamper
with my torn and ragged breath
and felt a shame that knew no bounds
and something underneath.
The shreds of rotten underwear
they were my very soul
and where I had a smiling self
I now had just a hole.
I never felt ashamed again
for decades since that day
the laughter and the cruelty
just took all my shame away
but neither could I feel the sun
accomplishments or joy
I was nothing but a cipher
now no more a little boy.
But I have changed my underwear
and I have changed my mind
the laundrywoman's gone now

and I'm no longer blind.
Friends want me back the way I was
they want me deaf and dumb
but I have outgrown self-pitying
I am no longer numb.
So if I'm not the fun I was
and now have work to do
I'm sorry, I must amend myself
I can't stay dead for you.

Lost Along The Thorny Path

Have you ever been lost among the thorns
the sky red from your fear
the way obscured by brambles
a twitch and yap, another sting
afraid to turn, afraid to stay?
You burrow through the stickered hedge
looking for a shortcut that never appears.
Where is God in this green mess?
Where is God?

Fox-hole prayers avail you nothing
the hedge is God. Free will is all thorns.
Somewhere between the red sky and your browned up sneakers
there is a calm. You cannot fix this by action.
Sitting still, surrounded with whorling cascades of bile colored whips
unmoved by your own lacerations
you envision yourself forever in this place
rain or shine, dark through dawn.
No, the light does not reveal,
you just slowly move and slowly peel
each claw-wired friend from your back, or your inner thigh
you work towards freedom from the inside of the maze.
Slowly the knot of barbs becomes straight,
each step toward release is backsliding
into the thorny grip.

Another calm, another peel, another step
Little-by-little the depth of the trap becomes shallower
each relapse less biting.
and finally, *finally*, the way out appears.
I have remembered the thorny path ever since.
But sometimes I still feel its unwholesome pinch
and wonder did I ever really leave?
Or am I standing there still, still as an eave?

Snow in October

When all trees become willows
and branches kneel to the ground
winter comes before Halloween
with the whirring, oceanic sound
of wet rain falling into pools
around forgotten footprints
turning Goosies into Yules.

Misbegotten spirit beings
reflected in the snow;
Jack-o-Lanterns light the way
as blizzard's innards glow.
Hollowed, hallowed harlequin
October's dress o'er-laced
with spidery strings of crystal flakes
masking Autumn's face.

The Secret Star

I can still feel cool air's haunches
twitching at the barren branches
though muddy, the ground continues solid
right up to the river, squalid.

The clouds phalanx from west to east
the farther bank a shadow of dark trees
my jacket cannot fully block the cold,
and nature makes me feel quite old.

I see arcane symbols in the branching swirls
of water, wind and wood, familiar curls
of truth that I no longer care to read
I did when I was younger, I believe.

And soaring over the water's sinking mud,
a silent bird who bypasses the flood.
from tree to tree he plies his curious way
what knowledge he retains he did not say

But off he flies my solemn silent teacher
he knows my path more so than any creature
he is the spirit divine that soars above
and greets me dark clad, as a grieving dove.

The moldy clouds give way to leaden black
the raven's gone but I can see his track.
The scene forlorn, the same as once was I
but you're my secret star now in the sky.

The Sylph

One spring two strangers met along the ever wandering Rhône
Both headed in the morning's gloom for silent Avignon
A beautiful maiden girl was one whose skin was cold as milk
Her eyes were ringed with fire and her hair as white as silk
The other was an old, old man who walked a crooked cane
She held for him a sheep gate as they met upon the lane

"The sun will rise within the hour," her greeting did entail,
"That is the way of life," he said, "I've never seen it fail."
"I'm glad to meet a friendly face upon the darkened road
and hope you'll walk beside me all the way to Avignon."
"Of course I'll lend you company until the sun appears,"
the maiden said and smiled a knowing smile at his fears.

"I had a fortune teller say that fortune I would meet
upon the road to Avignon my journey would complete.
She said that I would find out who would take at last my gold
for I have wearied carrying it and now am very old."
"Why would you speak of treasure to a stranger on the road?
You trust me with your valuables, your safety and your soul?"
"Ah, that is true. I trust," he said, "my hopes you do inspire."
"Then face thy fate," she said, "for you have met your first vampire."

"For centuries I've roamed the earth and taken as my due
any life that came my way, or that I set mind to.
Nor love, nor joy nor hope nor fear, I've wearied of those games
and Shakespeare, Newton, Stoker, all are naught to me but names.
You've seen your life's adventures; sorrow, satiety and love
Your crooked walk through all that's done, and now comes heaven above
I'll still be milking humans when the world comes to a close
But Avignon and dawn are gone, the frost your time has froze."

"Your life is forfeit, adieu the sun, for I am a vampire.
Your gold is blood, your hopes are gone, and now you will expire."
She bit his leathery neck, inhaled his life and he was dead,
while gorging on his last ebb, she saw light over her head
The spirit of her victim hovered over her dark deed
with pointing hand he smiled sweetly, and harkened to her heed.
The body cold and lifeless rose again as if alive
It posed its crooked stance and then his spirit leapt inside.

"You have indeed received my gold, my mission has gone right
and now you are transformed and healed and given mortal life."
The maiden felt her heart restart, her limbs were filled with blood
her claws returned to gentle hands, her breathing hard and good.
"God sent me down to rescue you from all this dark and filth
Now go your way a mortal maid, for you have met the Sylph."

Framed

The beach as canvas, you as object
My Picasso mind boxing you into segments
Roiling surf as Ocean's breathy might
The day and you and the sea air smelled as one
Dark manganese-tipped waves roll forward and collect
your hands and mine, in and out, legs intertwined,
in the water's pocket
As Sol's vast glare tinged azureous white.

You were so like a doe stuck in the sand
A frightened rabbit as I offered you my hand
Almost scared your face thought "What to do?"
But when we touched, I think a galaxy blew.

The day was like a gull's eye view
Communing, we were two halves of a clam shell
We swirled in the energy at Neptune's door
Crushing Desire's pearls in our naked hands
High up and far away from all we knew
Feel the alien-yet-familiar panorama
The crest embraced the rip tide more and more.

At last the sweet eternal day finds end
and down the beach our separate paths did wend
The ocean's cube is framed but never through
And I've not for the last time painted you.

Down Here in The Rabbit Hole

What a glory, the mind
That sees Caspian Seas in cloud formations
Escher in the corner of a Kandinsky.

Then passion for another human being
lights him up like a neon sign
deep within the glowing filament
gorgeous stained glass cinders
lit like the sun by the smile of God
admiring his own creation.

Clouds were moving in two directions at
once
Easternly: white inside-out curlicues
continents as geometric swirls;
Above: gay ruffles like gray Pollock paint
stains
drifting lazily northwards towards Polaris.

The sky is blue
down here in the whole of perception
lit by emotions, filtered through life's stream,
an ornate Fabergé egg
etched into you and me.

The Dream of the Mirrors

My looking glass held the King of Wands
Mercury's child, the setting sun,
his countenance wise, his eyes were dun
His walking staff made of palm fronds.

He pointed to a distant mirror
and in its face I saw much clearer
the stomping charge of angry hooves
the weight of histories on the move.

I saw the chalice and a lonely stair
Solemn duty's nervous pace
and like a haunt about the place
A woman of years was standing there.

Her face was veiled but shining eyes
alone revealed her silent sighs
Reflecting glass in her cupped palms
a million's wails she gazed down on.

She looked at me and at the man
who paced the floor in worry's grip
She let the solemn mirror slip
It vanished from her open hand.

His eyes were fire, his temper cold
her disregard made him feel old
the suffering world cried on apace
despite the loss of pity's gaze

He closed the book, removed the cup
another object there he placed,
his hat was cocked down towards his face
against the wind his collar up

Amidst the scene another reflector
showed a lone and nerved observer
clutching his pillow in a bible-choke
The glass fogged over, and I awoke.

The Moments of Our Life

The moments of my life
A few million left
I throw handfuls away on
Petty squabbles,
Theft when perpetrated on
One's self, is a crime
Of self-abuse
Let us make our moments
Of better use.

Poem for Yuthy2

I've lost the ability to make friends
like the last coin from a purse
so I have been running after shadows
trying to make them see me
the closer I get,
the dimmer they appear,
until I touch and they become smoke.

The pain of the shame I feel
at playing hopscotch
on the interstate again
is dimmed by confusion.
Whatever am I looking for in this sand?
The footprints have faded away.

I miss the rough of more tactile drugs
the hot pavement of desperation
of needing people needing me
who don't go on about
honesty and humility
over a wire to strangers.

"Life is a fever-dream on the soul of nonexistence"
                —Happy Hiram

A Poem Reviewed

I find it is bad, I find it is good
goes too many places than it should
I can't decide just to itch, or scratch
- heard your ambiguity, wrote this to match
If you find it annoying well I do too
It is singsong,
repetitive,
circular
and blue.

Meaning No Disrespect

Meaning no disrespect
You can't tell me what you mean
I am a special case
Because I am just an amateur—or—
I am simple folks—er,
I am just posting
for the whole world it's sent
But I didn't want you to read or
—God forbid—comment.

Meaning no disrespect
You can't criticize me
I am an endangered group,
I am in love
I have mental health issues
And health issues
and abuse issues
And HEALTH issues.

Thereby, I can write great stuff
But cannot benefit from ACTUAL OPINIONS
They don't increase my fan base.

Meaning no disrespect.
You are interfering in future sales.

And So, Let it Be Red...

by beth williams

Unbeknownst the Whether

unbeknownst to the fellow
sitting under the umbrella
below the dripping sky

feeling rather mellow
like an eleven pm Cinderella
before the de-slippered goodbye

above his hatted head
stretched from clouds of dread
where the fist of questions arise

as the rain fell and spread
the answers soon were led
to his amusing surprise

his once upon a diamond dream
faceted with that midnight gleam
would end in such a mess

t'was not the time for him to deem
or less he lands further upstream
why not that certain red dress

while he sits upon the bench
in hopes his fears the rain does quench
he missed the sweet reply

her touch, he melts, and hands unclench
his heart leapt back from yonder trench
below the dripping sky

Umber Ella and Her Pastel Tote

Dimmed now,
the glints from her flinted eyes
veil the story of her heart's demise.

He wasn't there…

Empty now,
Her glass, garnet filled, the second of three
that stretched the minutes into eternity.

He didn't answer…

Closed now,
Her cell phone, oddly twirling under fingers of frantic,
thoughts puddle to frets, less than romantic.

But he'd said…

Poured now,
Her third glass of to be sipped stop-the-clock bliss,
as umber lights dance in rain shadows, dismissed.

Did he really?

Defeated now,
The truth of his might, even less than his may,
bittered her wine; her silvered hope, it frayed.

She decided…

Standing now,
A love built on maybes, in pastel side road cafés
Fades faster than wishes of an un-bought banquet.

Relinquish

Nice straight rows
don't matter
if the wire grass
takes over, meshed
into the flesh of the garden,
choking all it touches.

The stuff probably
laughs as it's being
hoed, chopped, dug,
knowing that each
root dropped back onto
red clay soil can just
begin again.

Even the dirt doesn't let go
easily, clinging to this
nasty grass like a child
refusing to unsnarl her
fingers from the chains of a swing
at the park, still knowing
that sometimes
it is truly
time
to let go.

Brass and Bass

spilled, chilled, revealed
the commotion, a notion
that words are the ocean
where I'm left to drown

the lines never drawn
the crosses never shown
intersecting explosions
brass and bass
brass and bass

the time it takes to erase
the words that debase
taste the brass
shine the wrath
tongue fired and insistent
taming the distance
from lips to ears

feel the bass,
admit the chase
hasten the wilt, the guilt,
tilt the world
pitched low, undertow
brass and bass
brass and bass

consumed, the new melody
outshining the parody
incanting enchantments
finger strummed delights
ignite, clutch tight
to that reality
as I loosen
this hold
and
sing
while I wonder if the heat
from that rainbow

splashed across
my stainless steel sink
is enough
as the sun and the rain
break through
their own differences
into prism sentences

Why She Blushes

Believe the truth within his eyes
Languish the longing in trembling thighs
Understate ardor enjoyed with surprise
Simple captives between silken sighs
Hello won the prize, hello won the prize

Lingering moments, sideways stare
Understand, overboard, in between care
Sudden flushes caught unaware
Hello won the prize, hello won the prize

Sharing touched minutes passing untold
Hazily tracing placed hands in Love's hold
Uttering hints outlined in gold
Soaring heart room, intentions bold
Hello won the prize, that smile in her eyes.

Reflections from a Wind Chime

A sound of nature
made by man's hands
the wind chimes weave their spells
proving unseen forces
act, react, refract, attract, impact

often clamoring frantically
they rush together singing
of approaching storms
tinkling tonal warnings;
reverberations to come
trilling crescendos to ride
wave-like, breaking

vibrations, aural auras
remembered, reasoned
rhythmically recalled
that memory mixing
with the flats
these new thoughts
meshing with those sharps

when time is to be stilled
the counsel they whisper
in dulcet voices
calms the disquiet with
single slow pings of now…
here…
present…

each peal
removing layers of a rusted past
scaling a film of tomorrow
harmonizing a rest;
before we pick up
the cadence of
maladies and melodies
that underscore
our lives.

Exposed

Jagged,
raw edged
stumbling rocks

fingers gashed
on what
could have been

wrists streaked
muddy with the color of
what could be

arms bearing
pebbles of the past,
scattered like boulders

footsteps, scuffling
engulfed in fresh waves
of today,

exposing the
underside of tomorrow,
all flowing into...

Time
mixes
like blood
into the brine
of life;
the waterway
of both forfeit
and triumphs.

Red Deliciousness

"Quit it."

"sigh…"

damn
the dynamics
of a kiss
a shift
from the pride
in a Mother's purse
to the know
bestowed by
a beau;

like she bit
into the apple
again.

My Favorite Cage

So quiet,
collected,
here in my
cage, viewed by

all, yet catering
to the few
swept
moments I have

snatched
from the glory
lifted for a price
with vengeance

being the barred
outcry, so quiet
here in my
cage, skewed

the vision, of my
haughty love,
pecking away
at the order

of another
man's dream,
whose voice, is
never confined

still my broken
song, so quiet
here in my
cage, where

vanity reigns
crimson
stains the
veil, and slowly

I sing myself
to sleep,
crowned
with echoes of

what could have
been so quietly
here in my cage,
collected.

Waiting on the Bus I Always Seem to Miss

I didn't even know I was waiting.

Inside the tavern, a festival
of folk gathered,
pressing close,
after shaves leaving trails in cigar smoke,
rose scented wrists drawing
excited butterflies in mid air, all mingling
with ribbons of laughter,
easy speak, and charmed chiding.

Late, but elated to join the
revelry, I reached into the
throng, meeting new hands,
dancing to woven timbres, my laughter
tinkling like wind chimes chasing
home bound geese, in wonder
at new words released.

Last calls bounced down halls,
good byes grew dimmer, shading
the departing footsteps like
moth prints in windowsills.
My feet too, finally funneled through
the tavern door, tired, but inspired.

Not yet willing to call the night over,
drawing circle spells in the light snow
that dusted the sidewalk, I found
myself alone, beside a wrought iron
bench, echoing its chill. This time,
too late to rejoin the glimmering cloud of laughter drifting
towards…

Fists, like nubs, shoved in shallow pockets,
lingering for the bustle, that never ran my way,
I didn't even know what I was waiting…
for.

Sacred Carving

Love is

hieroglyphs
etched into a burning
log, seared with pleasure
branded with pain
where in the
embers
lies the sacred
mystery.

Long Sleeves Worn Over Hearts

"Why the jacket today?" I ask.
"I'm chilly." she says.

The deviant debutant
looks through
the broken window pane;
glass fragments seen…

not as
destruction
deconstruction
detriment
debris

but as
completion
contemplation
consciousness
covering.

"But the sun, it's warm today." I reply.
Shrugging, she mumbles, "I'm just holding back the cold."

Seedtime

Sometimes, I don't want
to write deep forest
endings to new fountain beginnings.

I'd rather visit
the heady scent of wisteria
that drapes the air
long after my walk has passed
the purple curtain,

where the at most feared
is clouded by that amorous
aroma;

making the vivid blue skies
meld into red tinged dogwood buds
of Spring, the greens, browns,
splotches of white painted pinks

patch working
the view
of the day.

compressed carbon caterpillar

by evadne anderson

Written in Stone

Wealth,
riches 'neath sapphire eyes.
Faceted emotion.
Turn me to Light; read Stories,
words I have written but do not understand.
Translate me, my Maker,
but do not forget…

My heart is a pigeon blood ruby,
dripping gems as I pour myself out.
Set me in bands of silver,
and gold,
wear my sorrow as Power and Truth.

Examine my soul, the Pearl of Great Price,
beauty formed around a flaw.
Test me between your teeth; feel chills,
I am real, hidden, and longing to be found for

my spirit is a diamond,
rough and untouched,
seeking another, seeking its Former.
I am crying
to be Cut.

Hercules

Dark world awash in acid taste,
bleak concrete city made of waste,
where broken things are forced to fly,
and where the mighty go to die.

They call us dragons, swift and strong,
endurance only lasts so long
but as we break they watch us cry
and say the mighty never die.

They tell us that we can't feel pain,
skin *doesn't* burn in acid rain,
so slave without good reason why,
lest rest permit the mighty die.

Freedom a word, forbidden, sweet,
so cloaked in chains with broken feet
I trudge the stairway to the sky,
no longer mighty, free to die.

Cicada

Look deep beneath my earth within,
slick shattered cell of ancient sin
from force to force, unrendered blame,
anomalies of guiltless shame,
dark roars of gods becoming men.

My mission clear, I raise my pen
to write this world anew again
and sacrifice my former name,
deep beneath my earth.

As universes twist and spin,
I live the moment I begin
to loose the soul God couldn't tame,
to break the rules of Heaven's game...
to shred this mortal shroud of skin
deep beneath my earth.

Laundry Day

Find me under piles of dirty laundry,
curled in a wrinkly ball.
No Tide to erase these tears,
no Shout to cover screams.

Bleach bleach bleach,
bleach for the tongue that speaks defiance,
spin cycle,
hot water, holy water,
"Lord, save this please, it's my favorite."

Bleached out skin, bleached out hair,
colorless waif stands,
fresh tumbled from the dryer.
"Do you like me now?"
"Am I pretty and clean?"

I'm sick of split nails from the washboard,
of skin rubbed raw with lye;
sick of the circle that's hotter than hell as a penance!

Shower me in dyes of vivid colors!
Let me roll in the mud, chocolate, and blood!
These stains are poetry and song,
deeper than my skin and in the end…
it doesn't matter if you see
where I have been.

Soot on a Wineglass

Color me in claret and in sin,
ash drips from my fingertips
I am internal rhyme.

Follow the red brick lick-scar road
into witch's eyes,
hypnotize, tantalize, euthanize…
fear free feel free free fall.

soot smudge mirrors,
ice white fog smoke,
blood bond blunders…
it's a dagger to the gut baby,
one I plunged into myself.

Maybe I'll find it again,
use that needle blade to stitch those wounds.
Until then…

Taste me.
Cloves and cinnamon.
Chocolate.
Precious, precious
pure and painful
pleasure.

Poet's War

Wrap me in linen,
incensed frankness and myrrh.
Thou shalt see me unearthed,
hold my heart in thine hand.

Weak weapon wielder,
wanton though winsome,
shame is the masque on the heart on the sleeve.

Secret-shined silver,
slipping through liplock,
truth mothers moments that twist in the knife.

Pieces of paper,
platitude plastered,
bandages twined 'round a world's worth of wounds.

Shedding skin armor,
let this war leave me damaged!
See me naked, unbroken,
shielded heart, shattered pen.

Smoke on Snow

Slow crescendo,
building in a mind unused to warmth,
foreigner to friendly words and light,
seamstress stitching canopies of night.

Music movement,
stillborn echo of that ling'ring dream,
prayer for more than evidence unseen,
Hope's melodious moonlight leaves it bare.

Naked dancer,
nipped by frost until the spirit shines,
crafting monuments in written lines,
effigies and whirlwinds, folded steel.

Vagrant memory,
returning now unto the soul to rest,
the mercy cavern carved within her breast—
upon a time I called that body mine.

Decrescendo,
leave her mind alight with fire's glow,
let her sleep amid life's chaos dream,
silhouetted shadow stamp on snow.

This Title is Not Your Name

There are dreams deeper than nightmares,
reaching into Soul,
twisting threads 'til the heart is a snarlball tangle.
I've spent days with reason, chaos,
and a seam ripper,
my own mind locked in itself like a pitbull's jaws.

I have stopped time to lock eyes with a black cat,
held Infinity,
a tiny, wounded hummingbird,
in my hands,
fallen in love at the blink of an eye…

I cease living to love life.

Open hearts cannot protect those with walls,
how could I have been so blind?
The song I sang for you was "Possession."
Funny…was that All you wanted?

Dear one,
my heart was not made for the leash but the lash,
spirit to be sliced asunder
by sacred shards of Beauty.

Simple Redemption

No name but Love shall touch my lips with reverence.

I will open my arms,
embracing your crosses,
bare my back to your whips as you whisper,

"The Heretic has come,
proclaiming a new God."

I wear chains and I wear fire,
the smile that is a sneer.
Face me, Universe,
see blue that dims your skies.

I have walked deserts with bleeding feet
and bladeless defied armies.
I swim the Seas of Doubt to drink of my own Fear.
I tremble, shedding tears greater than Grief.

Joy, for I have seen the face of God
in every man.
Joy, the Age of Prophets is reborn.
Laughter at the truth.

Truth is not the end pursuit.

Voiceless Night

Words lay concealed, quiescent,
like the bones inside my closet,
aching to be stretched with flesh,
infused with blood,
inflamed with breath.

Let me walk again in rain tasting of copper
as thunder cries the names of gods unknown.
Celestial transfusion,
let me wash myself in lightning,
for Heaven screams in pain that is my own.

Color me with violet 'neath the skin,
revealing ancient godhood locked within,
version of a life lived unabridged,
written as though wordlessness is sin.

I need never e'er have spoken,
let my living stand as witness,
unclothed as Nature is unclothed,
shameless as she is shameless.

Dream in the copper rain with me,
crack lips and eyes to taste and see
Life's banquet of unspoken words,
her dance of naked bones.

New Vows

Onslaught, onslaught, torment, torment,
bending, splitting, damage, ravage, rage.
Twisted spine, fractured shoulders, boiling blood.
This world is built of Pain,
I am besieged.

War drums beat, right hand lusts,
the left, subverted, knows—
among the willow branches no fortress can be crafted but…
could pliance be a different brand of strength?

Lives beyond lives forged the Warrior,
this ancient inner shrine,
an archaic angry god demanding blood.
No more. No more.
I battled for new breath yet
have not let my new heart move me.

Warrior, cede to Poet,
leave atonement to its time.
Love alone shall break me.

Manchester

Dare me.
Move me to a place beyond words,
under galaxies, through stars and the core of the macrocosm.

Say one tiny phrase,
distance enclosed by the littlest whisper,
the baby's hand clutching a finger controls.

I will silence.
I will dance in the void of my tongue ever stilled.
I will burn.
I will bring down a heaven and build a new earth.

Challenge me
with touches and kisses and thoughts
from blazing blue nowheres.

With one minute moment,
one fractional change, the poles are reversed;
signals collide.

I will sing,
weaving latitude longitude into a web
to hang from the stars, a celestial hammock
where my only companion is you.

Tempt me
with secrets and sorrows,
stories of scars.

One pattern broken,
with metal, fire, and ink,
hearts splintered to fragments of Gothic cathedrals.

I will build them again,
staining the glass of your heart with my blood.
I will mend you,
with wreath-fire promises filled by my love.

Legend in Another Time

Wish you were there wish I was too.
Sweat-smeared,
cracked hands,
concrete grit in my eyes,
I build the foundation.

Father tells me stories,
tales of my gospel given breath.

I dream of angels
and walk with gods made flesh,
yet not laid my hands inside those wounds
or heard the roaring whispers.
Never seeing—believing,
hoping truest faith is blind.

Seek me on moonless nights
when well and will run dry.
The stars are yours to fill your visions,
your futures prayers and scripture.

May your music never silence,
let your dancing never cease.
Always will I be here keeping
trust, blind faith, blind peace.

the thirteenth floor
(out on a ledge)

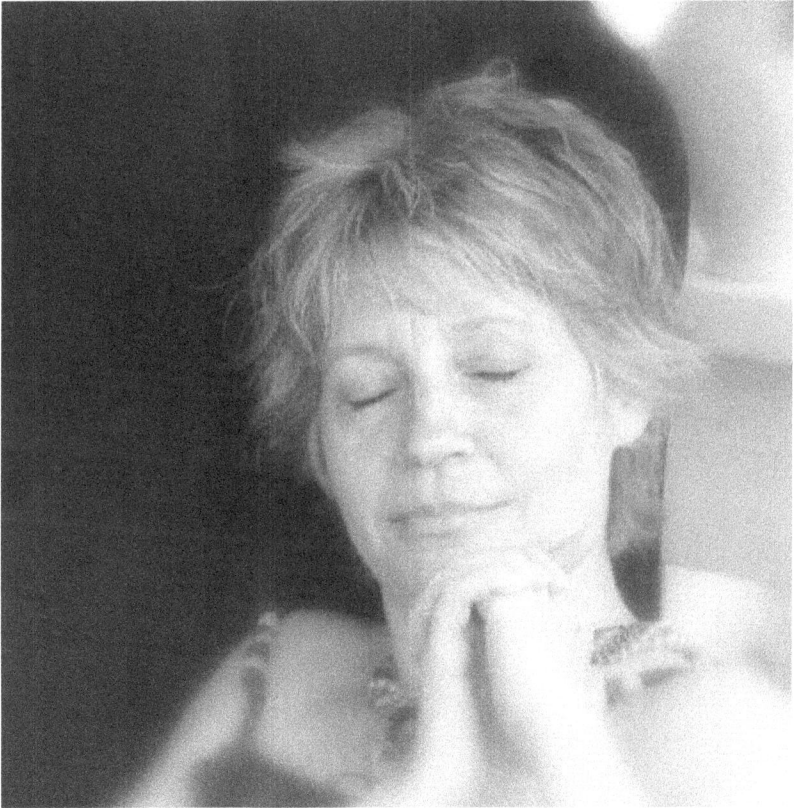

by nancy e. alcorn

Open Doors

I did not
set out to write
a book or
even a letter…
I only thought to
spend awhile
a message to deliver
I opened up the door, quite wide
to let in clean fresh air
I got down on my knees
to scrub, I should have
said a prayer
If you are out there
looking
and see me scrubbing
gently—
my thoughts on people,
places
things
I did not feel so empty
I raked the needles
in my yard
discarding evil
thoughts
by working up an
appetite, and angering
my muscles…a puzzle
a conundrum
it has me in its grip
as words slip off my finger tips
and hit
the noisy keys
panoply of—
and off I go in
some other direction
deflecting
and protecting self
as I have been
the chosen

a sitting duck
a carnival
you shot and hit the mark
leaving a dent and me all wet
was this your true intent?
where is justice?
where is truth?
I lost
…'twas something in my youth
glossed over
charged with grown up
moods and adolescent attitude
and
now
my mind is muddled
dense
my thoughts a mess
and I intent
on righting what is wrongful
but
…the web has come and set
her weave
perhaps will leave me comatose
inadequate, I do
suppose
deflate,
and wait
for second best

my goodness what was this about?
I wrote too much without a doubt
twisting, writhing worms
intent
on causing
my mind to be bent…

good morning.

A Bed Time Poem

as bedtime poems go
they can be about anyone or thing
so sit down children
and adults alike; as to you
this evening
I bring…
Sheep with Pink Bows

some of them blue…as
I cannot be certain
that pink's the right hue…
I put on some red ones and
pretty green also
so now I will get to the poem
I promised

counting sheep as they leaped over
serpentine fences
curled up on benches
in overgrown forests
…they were all bedecked
with colorful bows.
all of them lovely and here's how it goes

suppose you were lying
beside me in bed
and you could not hear
a word that I said
but I showed you in pictures
a tale I had drawn
of little white sheep
on a manicured lawn

well these lambs all got tired
but they knew you needed
to count as they jumped
and so all of them heeded your thoughts
and they now
in pink ribbons and bows

tore through the forest
where fairytales grow…
and low
and behold
they came then upon you

they ringed around rosie
a hullaballoo…
for Blue Children danced
in their nightgowns
and caps
the poor little lambs guessed
these kids must have napped
and they laid down in
silence to watch
the charades…
and soon were all sleeping

I think 'twas a trade
now sheep count the children
while falling asleep
…
so that is the way
that the tale has to go
because I am tired
and if you must know
when I come to tuck you
into your bed tonight
beside you I'll see a lamb
of black wool, not white
with a brilliant pink bow
tied around his neck curls
and a pink ribbon
in your hair
because you're my girl

As You Drift Off to Sleep

Flaxen hair on
fire
upon a silken slip of pillow
rests a sleeping head
Sunlight filters
through the blinds
firing up the flax
it looks like fairy dust
is sprinkled, dancing
in the dusk,
and in a
rocking chair
a bear
is singing
"Tura Lura Lura"

Outside the room
where slumber reigns
a creaking floorboard
mutters
as a mother goes about her
business
closing
all her shutters

sits down in a big arm chair
with a well-worn book
runs a calloused finger
across
inscription on
the page,
and in the
dying embers of
the sun at end of day
she closes it again
and both her eyes
she kneels to pray

A mother's love
will keep on going
on and on and on
Long after every one and every
other thing is gone
the cupboards empty
table set
with bowl and cup and spoon

Tomorrow dawns another day
their hunger in it looms

Good night

Lullaby Bye

Sleep, my love
a cloud cover over
as mother sings
a lullaby
hush now, let me see a smile
wipe away those salty tears
the years will tackle you
in no time you
will be a man, and I
your mother always loves you
no matter where
you stand
Tonight the stars
are holding court
in a seamless sea of
velvet
the lunar slice of
onion in the sky is dipping low
and I will croon in
silver tones a melody
of love
and lay you down
upon your quilt with teddy
watching over
rock you with
a prayer and kiss
before I
make my way to bed
and lay my weary head
upon a satin pillow
for a moment
and sleep will conquer me.

Seasons & Reason

He was springtime
bursts of fragrant remnants
interspersed with showers
chasing purple rainbows
in puddle's
eddied wake

She was autumn
fall like rhythm to her
subtle colors
reverberating in
summer's dying heat wave
dancing on the wall
of stone and
cement crumbling

He took her
breath
away from sudden winter
collapsed the
summer leaping to
her side...

and where did summer go,
could they forget the winter's chill
push forward
just to feel a thrill

he sprang
she fell
obsequious and insolence
met as they embraced
seasoning
the morning

they frolicked
in the sun.

**…all about me
or
…this is NOT about you**

Had been sitting on my
laurels
wasting time picking lint
exploring
in this vast desert of a mind
and pondering the meaning
of life

a novel notion crossed over
…a cirrus cloud
in a most secular
seclusion…this intrusion
intrinsically relates to my navel
obligations
and citations I have paid…
and I wondered
how much lint to gather
from this novel
concave surface

as I picked another bit
of lint
from out my belly button…

Power of Words

the words ran together
pelting her back
a driven rain
enveloped her in
a prismatic
moment
They stroked her ego
a blossom was formed
a torturous delicate satiable flavor
of something deliciously warm

then words became short
they felt rather terse
they unsettled things she had
meant to rehearse
In a burst they came flooding
Like some raging storm
Broke down her defenses
Leaving her open
To vultures and dinosaurs
Loose in her prism

On the back of a dragon
Took flight (she could run)
And ran to his arms
As if shot from a gun
Slipped off his back
Blew a kiss
as he spread his wings
Breathed fire and hissed
Disappeared in a mist of confusion
Was this reality or illusion

She looked up and saw them
Her heartbeat went cold
All the words gathered 'round her
Suddenly bold, they accused her
And railed at her making her shake
Caused her to run, once more
She would run and hide from

This thing which threatened
to take her
No longer a dream
it seethed
And it crawled
underneath her pale skin,
and
the words would again
Run wrapping around her
Like
Yesterday's sorrow they ran
And
they smeared on the page
That was laid loosely there
Beckoning her from the desk

The words were responsible,
They made this mess

Now she sits in a cubicle
Tries to confess, the words
Agitated and made her undress
The rest
Unrelated
The words reveled, drank,
had won once again
With this well thought out prank
while a girl in a strait jacket
Was wheeled out
And away

Then
The scent of a
blossom was again formed
a torturous delicate satiable flavor
of something deliciously warm

Between Two and Three

!—
it is
or was
might be
don't know, her breath
in spurts of air bursts loose
and curse the day
she took
the first
then plead the fifth
both drank her dry
and then
those filthy eyes
(would cry)
to do or die or in between
none of her life is so serene she
picks
and chooses—loitering
in alleyways
and in between
the lines upon her forehead
deep from squinting eyes to help her see
and looking into sun's bright stare
then screaming,
banshee in despair
No One
not one to pick
her up and coming
faltered, rocked
and wrapped within a blanket sits
with eyes glazed over
lost her wits.

Phillip

when I last looked
you were just a wee lad
but I turned around twice
and you were gone
grown out of all
that I had given
tossed to the side

I felt your eyes, the last time
we spent
that day…me packing
you with your camera
were you filming me
to remember?
I still to this day
look for your face in
crowded rooms
wondering who you've become
and if ever
you will come back
to me, your mother.

and so I sit
here at my desk
typing idly when sleep is
pushing me
claiming strangers
as my family,
brothers, sisters
a child so blue
but
what is lacking
you must know;
my son
is you

Buttons

Long sleeves
flitter,
gasping movements
fanned by mother
father raging
all the
buttons
broken loose
scattered
broadly on the scene

Sight turns
inward
travels slowly
wetness racing down
her spine
brawling winds
and sprawling limbs
and lack of song
from tiny birds
ominous
this sky has opened
gaping mouth
screams
as she whips
her fury overwhelming me
"and where
have all
my buttons gone?"

"Oh my!"

(fingers rubbing)
fabric torn
twisting bits
between her thumb
and
broken
pieces cover her
she cannot move

breathes in
breathes out
letting go…a tiny noise is
wiggling up

She feels it
from her very toes
emanates
a tiny squeak
from beneath
rubbles
piled heap

and wonders

"Where
have all
my buttons gone?"

Catatonia

She has me in her grips
tethered
intense
ribbons cutting,
many pretty colored ribbons
red stilettos
tempering the mood
dangling
obsequious, irreverent
bending
my knees

would you go there
with me?
or must I here alone
fight the forces facing me
atone
Is it to last the night?
or will it give relief
however brief
I grasp
while gasping, little puffs
of oxygen
or something else akin
to that perhaps it is just helium
as giggles
rack my frame

a shame you are not
here to see
the things I see
I see these things…
and seethe within my veins.

what have they done with me?
I scream
no legs, no arms
and in between
suspended from
a make-shift line, I see my brain…IT'S SO sublime!!

I give you this
it's part of me
and doing so
it sets it free

in cyberspace now flaunts
and flames
while wildly now
the games play out
I die out
over
and
out

You – Mine

You
Are to
Me as a
Cool breeze blowing
On my blushing cheeks
Cool, fresh, tantalizing
Stretching out my arm I seek
Life's extensions cool yet balmy
As starlight bathes and moon seduces
You are to me as a cool breeze blowing
Seduction, bathing, feeling produces
Security in where we're going
Warm dew kisses gently calm me
My two knees now becoming weak
Contentment realizing
On my blushing cheeks
Cool breeze blowing
Feels to me
Love is
Mine.

For My Sister

Sunlight, fled as raging rains,
flooded in, assuaged my pains
In flashes childhood, flickers brief
with dancing laughter, sweet relief
Would I have taken all that pain
made it my own, exchange or
share it equal, keep her here
near my heart so very dear.
My sister, my friend,
though passed on through
I hold the parts
(the best of you)

Elizabeth,
don't cry for me
I'm smiling now (if you could see!)
no more pain, floating freely
When light rains fall
recall my face
I am all right, remember now
we all must go sometime, somehow
hold your friends, your children close
recall my life, don't fret my death
in every breath you take, I will be there

forged by fire

meet the poets

Thirteen Poets...Stoked Up

Temerity, like an avalanche falling from their faces
Halcyon, a rose petal floating on a mill pond
Intensity, a glass of old cognac, consolation, direction
Repine, as history is rewritten
Temperamental, storms in otherwise undisturbed spaces
Elemental, like rip-currents and red-tide
Efflorescence not rain-bowed
Nuance of descriptive words applied

Protected behind stars, our fueled thoughts enter the Sun, torched yet unburnt
Onerous, weighted under a sheen-sickled moon
Etching, sketching, honing and wrestling words into swords
Tungsten edges, mended hearts, silent warriors with honor not forsaken
Serendipity takes over kindling; effecting delight—unsuspected pleasures.

Dave Magill

Dave Magill, who lived most of his life in Minnesota, now comes to you from the soggy Northwest where he resides with his wife, Patti.

He is the author of *The Difficult Questions*. Dave's tastes in poetry are diverse and his inspiration, as with most poets, comes from his own life experiences.

Dave recaptures and enraptures us with scenes in his poetry—scenes that, to the less artistic eye, may have been insignificant and quickly forgotten. When they are recalled with his unique style, they become ingrained inside our own heads, almost as though we had been there with him. His words can be a slap-in-the-face awakening or as gentle as a lullaby, but they are always honest, always pure, always Dave.

Thank you Dave and thank you Patti for sharing him with us.

Chris Shaw

I imagine Chris in her kitchen in England. She is sitting, a cloak of anonymity drapes scantily, allowing me to glimpse a fraction of my awakening. As my fingers tap out the keys on my notebook—eyes squinting like that of a tortoise who has been disturbed and awakes to see what all the fuss is about.

I imagine Chris in her kitchen. she is sitting there composing something new (children safely delivered to school) honing each poem into an artist's rendering in her usual rhymed and metered style, basing most of her poetry on personal experiences, giving us glimpses of her life. Married, she is raising her three grandchildren, which helps maintain her youthful outlook on life. After 40 years in employment, she is content to spend her time in the home. I feel blessed to have found and maintained a friendship with her that spans the hours and the distance between our countries.

Benny De La Cruz

Benny De La Cruz lives in the Philippines. Since he began his foray into poetry he has grown existentially into his own feel for the art. Happily married, he follows my online writing and is one of my staunchest supporters to encourage and push me forward. It was those qualities that led me to him and pulled him into the group of thirteen. If I had to use one word to describe him, it would be a difficult task, so I will come back to this—if I should find that word. As of now, I am being pulled back toward that state where I will find sleep and perhaps a dream worth chasing and casting in stone.

Bruce Noblitt

Who is Bruce? He is a man who teaches, trains, and mentors while at work. Bruce's creativity continues in the kitchen where he is an avid cook for his wife and two daughters. Part of his charm is entertaining us with written witticisms in the form of poetry, which is more driven by the effects of industrialism and urban decay, allowing the reader to form their own opinions through his nostalgic renderings. He lives in Pennsylvania and usually comes to us from his cell phone while stuck in traffic. His swarthy frame shadows any entrance, and he brings a semblance of balance with his dry sense of humor (which I sometimes mistake for something else, causing me to prickle). We co-exist online perfectly.

Saundra Schmidt

Saundra Schmidt is currently living in Las Vegas, Nevada with her husband, Tom, and is a student in the field of psychology with a focus on treating PTSD patients with alternative methods to pharmaceuticals. In this alone, she displays the largeness of her heart, the depth of her spirit, and the keenness of her mind. She shares all of that with us here, with vibrant forays into places some would consider too dark to venture. She will always leave you feeling comforted, no matter the gritty content of her words. Her poetry is raw emotion that reaches deep into our hearts. Both her joy and her pain flow freely in her pen, in equal measure where we can feel them with her. She has grown her poetry in the last five years into a style that is all her own. As a fellow writer I hold her with my favorites.

Brian Mayo

I asked Brian to define poetry for me and this is what he said: "Poetry is like standing up in a canoe. You almost always have a good reason for doing it, but you're never quite sure how it's gonna turn out."

I have this mental image of him in his surroundings, a single guy, his house nestled into the tree line, in the country on a winding dirt road in Michigan, his dog, Sam, keeping vigil on the stray cats line up at his door waiting for a hand out. He loves working with wood and stone and is often found in his garage and many times at his pond, fed by the sandy-bottomed creek which meanders through his property. He is enjoying the solitude of nature, the taste of a cigarette blending with the scent of dark roast coffee sitting on a large puddingstone that occupies a place of prominence near his pond. An idle thought crosses my mind, I wonder if I could maintain my balance standing in that canoe.

Danté Camerlengo

Danté Camerlengo has a mind like a minefield of explosions that create a wonderful array, not only of poetry, but more readily the artwork which graces the cover of our book. He is a modest man who resides in Marysville, Ohio, and one day I hope to hang an original of his artwork on my wall. For now I am content to dice and splice words with him from a distance. While he tells us he is not a poet, I disagree; we are all poets, in some sense of the word, and saying otherwise does not make it truth.

Frederic Parker

Frederic Parker—this man is a source of comfort in a stormy winter. I have never observed him raise his literate voice to cause harm. Rather, he protects and covers with a strength I admire. Married with two grown children and one grandchild, I can almost visualize him sitting on a porch swing with his beautiful wife, watching the sunset together. He says he is "a common man whose ambition in life is to live it well and never look back…unless."

I say he is far from common; he is our knight in times of darkness when our worlds go topsy turvy.

Elizabeth George

Liz, our only Canadian poet, lives in Ontario.

I have known Liz for a lifetime—the four years we have been through seem more like a decade of changes and growth. Describing her should be easy, one would think. However, I will only say she is a contradiction, an anomaly who needs to be taken seriously at times, while understanding her sense of humor and that her timing is in line with ours. I should ask Dave a bit about Liz.

Dave?…

Liz… I'll tell you ..She has a style and demeanor which demands attention. When you read her poetry, you'll know. It is some of the only poetry out there that actually applies to almost every reader. It is incredibly universal, while remaining specific enough for us to see the images and walk right into the verse with her.

Happy Hiram

Happy Hiram is the internet creation of Harry Lowry. Hiram lavishes faint praise and ill-conceived scorn on many poets and friends in online poetry forums regardless of their merits or his lack of critical ability. In other words, he calls them as he sees them.

Harry Lowry is a ne'er-do-well in his mid-fifties who has been writing (badly) for more than 40 years. He was a problem student (slow reader), a college drop-out, and spent much of his adult life unemployed and occasionally homeless.

He now works in the social services field, helping the homeless. Go figure.

There are some who feel he has a talent for poetry, although Hiram himself would call it "trite-cliché-ridden doggerel". But I guess we can allow the reader to judge that for her or him self. Harry hopes that Hiram proves at least a little worthy of inclusion with these other, more stellar poets.

You can find more of Hiram's poetry at his own website http://heliconhaven.blogspot.com.

Beth Williams

Busy, busy, busy. I call her Busy Mizzy, her real name is Beth. In her own words: "I dove into stringing words together into chains of sense, or scents, depending. I began seriously writing poetry, after meeting a group of online writers."

First and foremost she found Dave Magill, then others (yours truly included) who encouraged and critiqued all in the name of fun and creativity.

To me, she personifies Southern with all its soft gentility combined with rugged femininity and just plain hard work. When she and I hang out it is usually hiking through the woods and playing in the creeks, or just sitting on a log, contemplating what we see and smell. Although this has never been reality it remains a concept in my brain. I wish she could slow down a bit and sit a spell today, join me in a spot of lemonade or sweet tea, unsweetened for me.

Evadne Anderson

I imagine the youngest of our group, Eva, has already started her day. Also known as Evadne Anderson, a C-130 aircraft mechanic, she joined the U.S. Air Force after her sophomore year of college. Coming to us from Arkansas, we have both wandered in the same graveyard in the same small town. We share an inexplicable bond and, to me, her poetry is a pulse beating strongly—the depth of which is immense. Greatly misunderstood throughout her childhood, she has earned our respect and has two other books to her credit. *Inkscars* and *Enter the Ellipsis*, both books of poetry. She has also finished two novels, and is working on a third in pursuit of publication.

Nancy E. Alcorn

The English language is beautiful. It trips off of the tongue, and there are so many words with similar meaning. I tried typing "free spirit" into a thesaurus, and this is what it came up with.

"Beatnik. Eccentric. Flower child. Free thinker. Maverick. Nonconformist. Original. Radical."

And yet, in all these words, I can find no single one that encompasses the spirit of Nancy Alcorn. She took it upon herself to introduce all of us to you, and I have volunteered for the daunting task of introducing her.

Nancy and I have walked under the same trees, marveled at the beauty of the same skies, and danced in the same graveyards, even though our experiences were years apart. She has become a friend and sister to me over the years. She has lived in both the United States and Canada, and she currently resides in the state of Alabama. Her life has been fraught with much difficulty, including a divorce and a battle with Lyme disease. And yet, through all of this, she continues to look at life with a decidedly optimistic point of view.

Her poetry is the very definition of "free spirited." Grammar is toyed with as a cat with a ball of yarn, entrancing, lilting off the tongue and pleasant against the ears. Her subject matter spans a vast array, ranging from the beauties of nature to the humor of this life-experience, from the joyous moments of existence to deep, personal sorrows. Nancy runs the gamut of the experience of living.

Through thick and thin, she has stuck by this project, helping to drive it forward and see it to its hard won completion. I am proud to see my work stand alongside hers in this undertaking.

by Evadne Anderson

Afterword

Blending in my brain, strange figures in the mist reach out and beckon me, the completion of this book, the preface and the premise; I take none of this lightly, it has fallen to me to push to that end as I pushed from the beginning. The culmination of our efforts wants to be heard.

Absurdly, a pack of words tap me on the shoulder, threatening to upend me and push the books down neatly like so many dominoes. They say "you are boring your readers;" I say, "NOT!" and swipe at them with a spastic movement before rearranging my thoughts and retreating from the page. I will come back to this but I tire of the effort of breaking my concentration. As the sun rises over this small town in lower Alabama, I head to my kitchen to find a spot of tea.

These early awakenings are bothersome, in those hours between the light when darkness is at its deepest I toss restlessly—ensuing arguments internal to me, a toss-up as to who will win. Today, I did not win, sleep is not my prize. Thoughts like stoplights cause my writing to be difficult, at best, wanting to hold you in fascination, yet realizing that it is not in my power. It is not I, but the words which dance or dribble on the page. I realize our circle is complete; I was born and raised in the soggy Northwest, and this is where 13 runs back into one and we become a cohesive ball of personalities. We are complete, maintaining our autonomy over our personal destinies, becoming who we will be…

The common thread which joins us all is an early inception into a world of words that move to a beat and in such a fashion as to charm the reader.

Our love of this art and our need to express it and give it to you, the world large or small, to rip into, criticize, internalize, or just ponder, and I leave this book challenge now, handing it off to the one who would provide the final process, and wait impatiently for the day I can hold it—not the world's greatest nor the worst—leaves embedded with emotion, nestled between the coverlets not just once but 13 times over in a loving fashion. Enjoy!

Nancy E. Alcorn
Author of *Francine: Silk Stockings & Red Stilettoes*

INDEX

www.ingramcontent.com/pod-product-compliance
Lightning Source LLC
LaVergne TN
LVHW051046080426
835508LV00019B/1736